Making Peg Dolls & More

toys that spin, fly and bring sweet dreams

Hawthorn Press

Published by Hawthorn Press, Hawthorn House,
1 Lansdown Lane, Stroud, Gloucestershire, GL5 1BJ, UK
Tel: (01453) 757040
Email: info@hawthornpress.com
Website: www.hawthornpress.com

Cover photograph © Margaret and Paul Bloom
Photographs by Paul Bloom
Illustrations by Anette Grostad
Design by Lucy Guenot

Printed in China by Everbest Printing Company Limited 2018.
Printed on environmentally friendly paper manufactured from renewable forest stock.

Every effort has been made to trace copyright holders of extracts reproduced in this book. The publisher apologizes for any errors or omissions and would be grateful if notified of any corrections that should be incorporated in future reprints or editions of this book.
The views expressed in this book are not necessarily those of the publisher.

Hardback edition first published 2014.
Paperback edition first published 2018.
British Library Cataloguing in Publication Data applied for.

ISBN 978-1-912480-02-9

Making Peg Dolls & More

toys that spin, fly and bring sweet dreams

Margaret Bloom
Photography by Paul Bloom

Hawthorn Press

To my parents,

who have shown me

their love in so many ways.

And when you work with love

you bind yourself to yourself,

and to one another, and to God.

And what is it to work with love?

...It is to charge all things you fashion

with a breath of your own spirit...

Kahlil Gibran

Contents

Simple Projects

Toys that Spin & Fly

Herbal Comforts & More Sewing Projects

Foreword

As so much that is fragile in our technological world, the domain of childhood is endangered: play is quietly disappearing from children's lives. Yet, play is the heart of childhood and childhood is the soul of humanity! The young child's drive to play is innate; it is the root-force of well balanced child development. Through play the child makes meaning of her world, life makes sense! And the senses are the fundamental tools the child uses in this pursuit of meaning. Children not only make sense of the world they interact with; of equal importance, through play they also have direct impact on this world. They experience themselves as fully empowered partners in the give and take of life.

Unlike many sense-depriving toys, interactive screens and other products marketed to young children, which actually stand between the child and the true exploration of our beautiful green earth, this little book is an antidote and a balm! The child's senses will come alive while working with wood, wool, paint and felt! When complete, the doll will offer the empowerment of wish-fulfillment, having any adventure the small child can imagine. Certainly in the 21st century the clarion call for a new education is Creativity. Is creativity not the art of Imaginative Play, all grown up? Creativity is cultivated in hours, years really, of child's play. Like play, it is flexible, intuitive, trusting, self-initiated and directed, responsive to the present yet inspired by the invisible.

It is fitting that Margaret Bloom has quoted Kahlil Gibran on her frontispiece. Perhaps it is not immediately apparent that all work is 'Love made visible,' but all handwork made for, by and with children is the embodiment of the love between the child and the helping adult. One year, in my Kindergarten class, I invited the children's parents to participate in a doll-making workshop. I planned that they make a small doll for their child, one that, like these beautiful peg dolls, did not require great amounts of skill or time. At the end of two and a half hours each child had a little symbol of their parent's love, dressed in colorful felt. Fittingly, we called them the childrens' 'lovies.' At morning, each child walked through the door and ran to fetch their doll from the 'lovie basket.' Doll accompanied child throughout the whole day: sailing in a toy boat, inhabiting a castle, carried in a pocket, whispered to at nap time! These dolls were imbued with love and imagination. They were deeply rooted in the parent-child bond. And they, because of the child's imperative to play, had the wings of the child's creativity to carry them aloft.

With this book in hand you, also, can give your child a little taste of this real magic, a strong brew of love, commitment, thread, felt, and flights of inspiration. The small act of making toys with and for your child not only offers her years of imaginative play, but in its own subtly powerful way reclaims childhood for future generations.

Sharifa Oppenheimer 2014

Preface

When the first *Making Peg Dolls* book arrived in my craft shop in Nailsworth, Gloucestershire, all of us were instantly captured by the charming and inspiring way that Margaret Bloom managed to turn the simple craft of doll-making into an art form and a labor of love. Many of us had seen or even possessed our very own little peg dolls but nothing compares to the purposefully designed and meaningful 'wee wooden folk' which Margaret Bloom introduced to us in her book. These wooden dolls have brought endless joy to my customers (children and adults alike) and have encouraged many people around the globe to make their very own peg dolls.

My passion is to get people crafting, and almost daily I hear customers say that they are not creative. I believe wholeheartedly that EVERYBODY is creative! In my experience, many people are led to believe at a young age that they are not creative and lack the skills to create. A thoughtless comment may have been made by a teacher, parent or grandparent. I have heard stories where a child did not quite follow the instructions of a teacher but ventured out on their own to then come up with something a little bit different from what was expected. A child's belief in his or her creative ability is all too quickly squashed by a shaming comment, with consequences that go on into adult life. As a mother of four I too have had to adapt. When I set out for the first time to do some biscuit baking with my very young children, I had it all mapped out in my own mind: the perfect biscuits to be presented to their

dad in the evening after an afternoon of harmonious togetherness! I remember my despair when I realised that my children had very different ideas about how to make the biscuits. I realised that I had to let go of any expectations I had, and just LET THEM BE! Any intervention from my side should have been aimed at supporting *them* in bringing *their* ideas into fruition, and not my own. So our first biscuits were perfect little piles of shapeless dough!

When children craft with their hands, it is primarily about the creative process that takes place and only secondarily about the finished outcome. As adults we have probably learnt at some point to always finish one thing first before starting another.

Children create in the moment, and not finishing a project is not a big deal to them unless they worry about an adult's judgement. I strongly believe in the importance of letting children BE in the moment. If we can do that, their creative confidence is sure to blossom and bloom!

This new collection of peg doll and sewing projects by Margaret Bloom is perfect for children and adults alike. There is something for everyone: the perfectionist who wants to copy every detail; the inspired who may need a little encouragement to go on creating; the teacher who is looking for small, manageable and economical craft projects; the parent who wants to craft with, or for, children; and any child who wants to make their own little friend. I can't think of a more versatile craft activity that suits all ages and skills. As someone who has recently written a craft book on needlefelting (*Making Needlefelted Animals*, Hawthorn Press), I truly appreciate the creative inspiration, care and discipline it has taken to write such a widely accessible, inspiring and contemporary book. It is a pleasure to leaf through this colourful book and be inspired by the simplicity of these creations, which can only have come from the heart and a place of love; love for children and for the spirit of curiosity and creativity. So, this is my message to anyone who is going to make a peg doll: Feel as free as a child and enjoy the process, wherever it takes you. The outcome can only be perfect.

Steffi Stern

Author's Introduction

Since the release of *Making Peg Dolls* in early 2013 I have been touched by the kind notes and sweet photos of peg dolls created by readers from all over the world, but there is one letter which has never been far from my heart and mind during the time I have been working on this second book. The letter was written by a mother who told the story of a peg doll made by her young daughter in the image of a classmate who had died suddenly. Her daughter brought the peg doll she had created to school and placed the doll on the desk of the little boy who had passed away. Here is the rest of the story as told by her mother:

Something truly magical happened when the peg doll was placed where the little boy had sat in school. The children in his classroom started to interact with the peg doll, and children who were finding it hard to talk about their friend, talked to the peg doll. The children sat with the doll and he was hugged and cradled in little hands. The teachers were amazed and touched by what was happening. They were overcome and saddened by the tragic loss of this lad, and to see the children coming to terms with him passing by means of this peg dolly was meaningful and very touching. I was in tears when the school told me.

The peg doll now stands on the memorial table. I have been told by some children that the peg dolly is looking after all the tributes left on the table. The little doll will then be put in a memory box for the parents of the lad and his family.

Prior to the birth of my elder son I worked in the field of counseling and often used therapeutic art in my work with patients, but I find this story especially tender in the way such love and healing was brought forth through the hands of a young child.

In light of this story, and in tribute, Hawthorn Press asked me to include within this book a project specifically focused on comfort and healing. And so I created a Rainbow of Herbal Comfort Friends. These dolls can be made for anyone who needs a reminder of love and light; the dolls are small enough to be carried in a pocket, and, with a bit of assistance, these tiny dolls can even be stitched up by a young child (later on in this book you can see a doll created by my 10 year old son for my own mother).

In addition to the herbal comfort friends, within this book you will find a range of projects which appeal to various skill levels. Many of the toys require sanding wood and painting (perfect tasks for the small hands of young children) while other projects are designed for the skill level of an older child or adult. Additionally, most projects can be completed within an hour or two. As the mother of two young children, my own time for creative work is limited, and so keeping the projects small and manageable was a consideration. However, a larger consideration was this – I wanted to bring peg dolls off the shelf and out of the doll house to spin, fly and travel about in the larger world. Between the covers of this book you will find patterns for dolls to sit on your pincushion and help mind your stitches, dolls flying through the air on dragons and bright winged birds, dolls to accompany children through the day as they face the world and through the night as they dream on their pillows.

Whether you are making something for yourself, or handcrafting gifts for friends or a beloved child, I hope these little dolls will twirl and fly their way into your heart, and bring joy and comfort wherever they are needed.

Materials and Techniques

Peg Dolls and Other Wooden Pieces

Natural, unfinished wooden pieces are usually not expensive, and I tend to buy in bulk so that I have extra supplies on hand for my next project (after all, if one spinning top is fun, why not make 3 or 4 or 5?). Most craft supply stores stock a variety of plain wooden shapes; however if you cannot find wooden pieces in your local shops, there is a resource guide at the back of this book listing places where you can purchase peg doll bases and a full assortment of wooden pieces for every project in this book via mail order.

I have used five different sized doll-bases for the projects in this book: 6 cm (2³⁄₈ in) standard wood-people pegs, 5 cm (2 in) angel-pegs, 4 cm (1⁵⁄₈ in) boy-pegs, 3 cm (1³⁄₁₆ in) tot-pegs and 3 cm (1³⁄₁₆ in) baby/bee-shaped pegs. If you have purchased doll-bases which do not match the sizes or shapes of the wooden bases I have used, you can simply adjust my designs to fit your dolls.

Additionally, there are a number of other wooden pieces such as wheels, wooden beads and dowels used for projects in this book. Specific measurements for each of these wooden pieces can be found within the supplies list at the start of each of these projects.

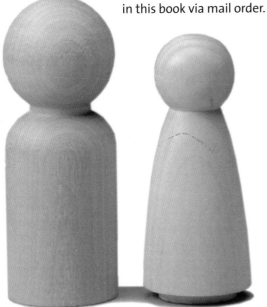

Woodworking tools and hardware

I must admit, I have always felt intimidated by woodworking tools, but every time I use them, my confidence grows. That said, the woodworking tools required for projects in this book are fairly basic – ones you might already own and use with confidence. However, if you don't already have the following tools, it might be worthwhile to purchase them to have on hand for future use.

For projects requiring dowels (the spinning tops, firefly rod puppets and wall hanging play-scapes) you will need a **small saw** to cut the dowels to size. Any

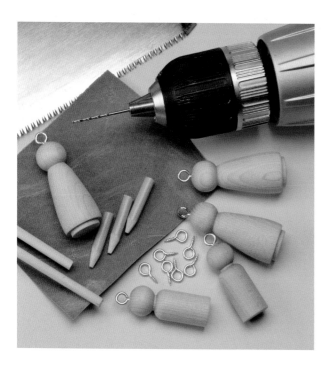

sort of small saw will do – I use a carpentry pull saw, but a folding saw, a jab saw or hacksaw will work just fine. After you use your saw, you will also need some 220 grit sandpaper to smooth the edges.

The next tool you will need is a **handheld drill** and a 1 mm (1/16 in) drill bit. These items will be required to drill holes for screw eye rings for the necklace, holiday ornament and hanging mobile projects. The silver screw eye rings I use on my projects are 13 mm in total length (US size 216½).

And for your safety, you will need a **woodworking vice** which clamps to a table or work bench. I cannot state strongly enough how important it is to protect your fingers by placing small wooden pieces in a vice when using a saw or drill! In addition to a vice, you may want to invest in a set of plastic vice jaw pads. I was frustrated when our metal vice damaged my peg dolls, and so I purchased a set of plastic vice jaw pads. The vice jaw pads were inexpensive and work like a dream – my dolls are no longer dented and damaged after a trip to the woodworking bench!

Finally, if you are planning to create spinning tops, you will require a **pencil sharpener**. Does a pencil sharpener qualify as a woodworking tool? Maybe, and maybe not, but I can assure you that a pencil sharpener is the quickest way to get points on the tips of your tops.

Paint and paint brushes

I currently use a **12-tone watercolor pan set** to paint my dolls, and I also keep on hand a few bottles of acrylic paint in basic tones – white, black, red, yellow, blue, plus gold and silver. Depending on your personal preferences, any type of paint will do as long as it is non-toxic; more important are your paint brushes. I own many paint brushes, however, I only use two of them – a very tiny, **fine point round brush** for painting small details and a somewhat **larger round brush** for painting hair and clothes on the dolls.

Colored Pencils

To be sure of eye placement, I like to create small pencil marks before applying paint. Other times, I might want to create a face with a softer look and so I draw the face with a pencil instead of using paint. Drawing faces on the dolls with pencil is also a useful technique for any child who worries he might blot the face by using paint. It's much easier for school age children to draw a face with precision using a pencil than to create a tiny face with paint.

Wool felt

Wool felt comes in many gorgeous colors and has a fine texture which cannot be imitated by synthetics. It is more expensive than synthetic felt; however, for tiny doll projects you don't need very much. For the larger projects in this book, you would require only half a meter in a few colors, and should have plenty of scraps left over to use in smaller projects later on. If wool felt is not available in your local shops, you can check the resource guide at the end of this book for a list of places where you can purchase it.

Glue

Any type of thick, **all-purpose, craft glue** (i.e. **PVA** glue) which is non-toxic and clear-drying will work for most projects in this book. I used **wood glue** for several items; however, if you don't have wood glue on hand, PVA glue will work just fine. I would also like to caution you against using hot-glue. PVA craft glue takes a few minutes to set and dry, enabling you to reposition items if you choose. Because hot-glue dries very quickly, it's difficult to make adjustments once items have been attached with it.

Sewing supplies

I use **six-strand cotton embroidery floss**, which is available in every color imaginable. Unless otherwise indicated, I have used one or two strands separated from a six-ply strand for all seams and embroidery in this book. As for needles, I use what is commonly referred to as a **standard embroidery needle** in size 8 or 10. Standard embroidery needles are available in sizes 1–12: the larger the number, the smaller the needle. Smaller size embroidery needles are especially nice when adding beads to a project (as I did on my pin cushion design) because the eyes of these small needles are narrow enough to pass through seed-beads; this makes it possible to embroider and add beads contiguously, without having to use a separate beading needle. However, children (and anyone who is just learning to embroider) may prefer using slightly larger needles as larger needles are easier to control.

A good pair of **fabric scissors** is essential for many projects in this book and a set of **pinking shears** can come in handy for cutting little crowns and embellishments. I have also recently added a **rotary cutter,** a **self-healing mat** and a **clear ruler** to my craft arsenal. The cutting mats and clear rulers sold alongside rotary cutters are marked with gridlines which make the task of measuring and cutting larger pieces of fabric a dream; this was especially helpful when I was cutting felt for the wall hanging projects in this book. That said, I have survived this long without a rotary cutter, self-healing mat and clear ruler. If you don't have these items on hand and are not inclined to buy them, don't worry. Just go ahead and cut your fabric with a nice, sharp pair of fabric scissors!

I only brought out my **sewing machine** for two projects in this book: the *Herbal Dream Pillow* and the *Snail Rider Gathering Bag*. Every other project in this book is sewn by hand. The *Dream Pillow* and *Gathering Bag* are both small and could be sewn by hand, too, if you do not own a sewing machine.

Beeswax polish

Using beeswax polish on your dolls is optional. When watercolor paint dries on the wooden bases it will have a soft matte finish. Giving your painted surfaces a good rub with a little bit of beeswax polish will make the watercolor paint transparent so that the wood-grain shows through, and it will also give the surface a delicate sheen. However, I never use beeswax polish on the faces of my dolls as it can cause the paint to smudge.

To make your own polish, heat a small amount of beeswax in a double-boiler along with some jojoba or olive oil. Once the wax has melted, you can pour the wax/oil mixture into a small glass jar or metal container and allow it to cool. The usual ratio of beeswax to oil is 1:3 (the beeswax being the smaller amount) but you can adjust the ratio according to your own preference. This polish will keep for a long time, and because it's used in small amounts, there's no need to make large quantities. To apply the wax, place a small amount on a soft piece of cloth or paper towel and rub. Continue rubbing, and finish the process using a clean section of cloth. You will know you are done when little or no paint residue rubs off on the cloth.

Wool roving

Wool roving comes in many beautiful colors and is easy to work with. I have used wool roving to enhance only two projects in this book, however needle-felting techniques are always handy for adding embellishments. Once you have mastered the technique, you will find that needle felting can be substituted for embroidery or appliqué anywhere a bit of detail or embellishment is desired.

For the needle felting enhancements on the projects in this book, you will need not only a **single felting needle**, but also a **multi-needle felting tool**. This tool will enable you to mesh the wool fibers of your roving onto a base fabric over a large area. Also, please know that if you choose to use needle felting techniques, you should always support your needle-felting work on a piece of **thick foam** to avoid stabbing yourself. Additonally, felting needles are very sharp, and children should always be well supervised when using them.

Extra supplies and embellishments

Other supplies you might want to have on hand are: pipe cleaner wires for the *Herbal Comfort Friend* project; some ribbon, colorful twine or cord for stringing necklaces; and origami or other craft paper for creating butterfly wings. Additionally, glitter, beads, bits of lace, tiny bells, feathers and seashells are lovely to have available, as well as acorn caps which can be used as tiny hats for peg dolls, and millinery flower-stamens for antennae. While none of these supplies are absolutely necessary, a cache of embellishments can be fun and inspiring.

Choosing a project

Within this book, you will find a range of projects which appeal to various skill levels. Some of the toys require sanding wood and painting (perfect tasks for young children) while other projects are designed for the skill level of an older child or adult. It follows that the projects which are easier to create will also take less time to complete, while the more difficult projects will require more time.

To help you choose your project, each is marked with one, two or three leaves:

 One leaf will indicate a very easy project. An adult might need to assist with drilling a hole for hardware (such as in the zipper-pull and necklace projects) but otherwise this is a simple project to complete.

 Two leaves will indicate an intermediate level project, which requires slightly more advanced skills.

 Three leaves will indicate projects where intermediate or advanced sewing skills are required.

In addition to this rating system, each project will include a section listing the portions of the project which can be completed by **small helping hands** (i.e. young children). Reviewing the information in this section might further assist you in choosing projects.

A NOTE ABOUT
THE PATTERNS IN THIS BOOK

Most patterns in this book appear in their actual size. Other patterns which need to be enlarged prior to use are clearly indicated. For the purposes of your own projects you may trace patterns or scan them and then print them out. These patterns and toy designs are for personal use only. The projects in this book are not intended to be made for commercial production or sold for personal gain.

Glossary of Stitches

This is a list of needle-stitches I have used on the projects in this book. There are many variations of embroidery stitches and, if you prefer, you could substitute other stitch designs for the ones I've suggested.

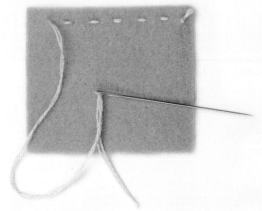

RUNNING STITCH
This basic stitch can be used to attach two pieces of fabric together or to create a gathered area.

BLANKET STITCH
This stitch can be used to create a decorative edging or to attach two pieces of fabric together.

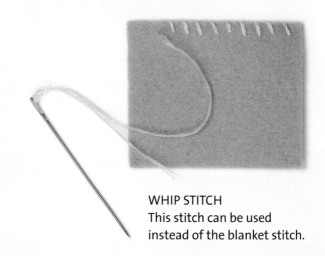

WHIP STITCH
This stitch can be used instead of the blanket stitch.

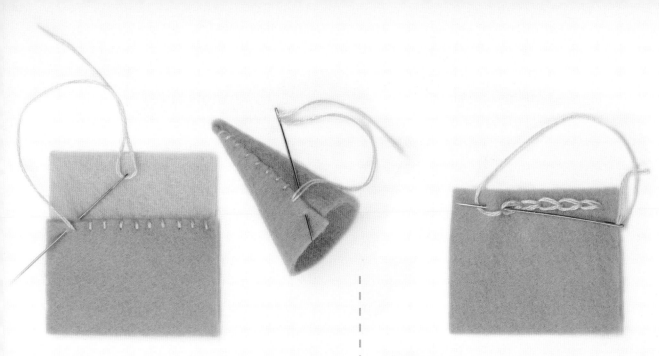

FELL STITCH
(Also referred to as APPLIQUÉ STITCH)
This stitch can be used to create a flat seam where one piece of fabric is overlapping another (as in overlapping fabric to create a cone-shaped gnome-hat). However, I use fell stitch primarily for attaching one decorative piece of fabric onto a larger piece.

CHAIN STITCH
1. Bring your needle through the fabric, from the wrong side to the right side, and then reinsert your needle at the spot where your thread is emerging. Before pulling the needle all the way through the fabric, bring the tip up again, a short distance away, where you wish to anchor your daisy-petal loop.

2. As you pull the needle through to the right side of the fabric, slip your needle through the loop of the thread so that the loop will be caught as you continue to pull the thread all the way through. Use the point at which your thread is now emerging to start your next stitch, thus linking your stitches together.

3. Continue your chain of stitches, and finish by anchoring the final loop with a small stitch.

DAISY STITCH

(Also referred to as DETACHED CHAIN STITCH)

1. Bring your needle through the fabric, from the wrong side to the right side, and then reinsert your needle at the spot where your thread is emerging. Before pulling the needle all the way through the fabric, bring the tip up again, a short distance away, where you wish to anchor your daisy-petal loop.

2. As you pull the needle through to the right side of the fabric, slip the thread under the needle so that the loop will be caught as you continue to pull the thread all the way through. Finish by anchoring your loop with a small stitch.

FRENCH KNOT

1. Bring your needle through the fabric, from the back. Starting near the center of your needle and moving in the direction of the needle-tip, wrap the thread around the needle two or three times.

2. Keeping the thread tight around the needle, slide the wrapped portions of thread toward the tip of the needle. Then push the tip of the needle back into the fabric a small distance from where the thread emerged.

3. Keeping the wrapped portions pressed close against the fabric as you pull, gently draw the thread through the wrapped portions to the back of the fabric.

STRAIGHT STITCH

The straight stitch can be used in many ways. Evenly spaced stitches can be used to form leaves, flowers and stars, and tiny stitches can be used to create a delicate face.

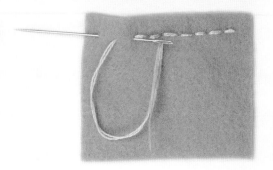

BACK STITCH

Bring your needle through the fabric from the back to the front. Reinsert the tip of the needle down through the fabric about 3 cm (⅛ in) to the left of where the thread is emerging and then up again 3 cm (⅛ in) to the right of your original starting point.

Pull the thread all the way through, reinsert the needle 3 cm (⅛ in) to the left, and then up again 3 cm (⅛ in) to the right of where the thread emerges from the fabric.

Doodle Page

I often make small sketches of my dolls before I set to work creating them. Perhaps you would also like to experiment with drawing faces and designing colorful costumes. Doodle away! Have fun!

Part One

Simple Projects

Stringing Beads & Spool Snakes

One of the most basic toddler toys is a set of stringing beads. This easy project can be created by anyone, but it is an especially nice craft for an older child to make as a gift for a younger sibling or friend.

SUPPLIES

Selection of large wooden beads in a variety of shapes (I suggest at least 7 of each size/shape so that there is a variety to play with!)

3.5 cm (1³⁄₈ in) sphere-shaped beads

2.5 cm (1 in) sphere-shaped beads

2.5 cm (1 in) or larger – cube-shaped beads

3.5 cm (1½ in) or larger – disc/wheel-shaped beads

5.2 cm (2 in) tall spools

1 cm (³⁄₈ in) bead (for the snake's nose)

Sandpaper (optional)

Heavyweight string, cord or shoelaces

Watercolor paint & brushes

Red and black pencils for drawing a face

Beeswax polish and a soft rag or paper toweling for application

PVA or white craft glue

Scissors

In our house, it is not enough to merely thread our beads together – the fun continues when we each grab the end of a long string of beads and take off running through the house. Much to the delight of my two sons (and to the chagrin of the cat), the bead strings make a happy clatter as they rattle along our wooden floors. This favorite game is how I came up with the idea of painting a face onto the head bead, then securing the beads in place to make an impromptu pull-toy snake.

The large-sized, plain wooden spools and beads required for this project can usually be found at craft supply shops. If the craft shops near you do not stock unfinished beads and spools, the wooden pieces can be purchased by mail order from shops listed in the resource guide at the end of this book.

SMALL HELPING HANDS

- - - - - - - - - - - - - - - - - - -

This is a perfect project for small helping hands! Most children over the age of three could help sand the beads, choose the paint colors, apply the paint and afterwards, help rub the painted beads with a little bit of beeswax. They could also help choose the pattern in which the beads will be strung and then string the beads for a snake. Setting up the nose for the snake and tying knots are the only steps in this project for which young children will need the assistance of an adult.

Painting the beads

1. Prior to painting, you may choose to give your beads a quick once-over with some sandpaper to smooth any rough portions.

2. Choose colors, apply paint to your wooden beads and allow to dry.

3. Using a paper towel, rub the beads with a small amount of beeswax polish. This will remove excess paint, preventing it from rubbing off onto little fingers when the beads are played with.

Stringing a wooden snake

1. Cut a piece of heavy string or cord approximately 2 meters (78 in) long. Coat the ends of your string with a little bit of PVA or white craft glue and wait 10 minutes for the glue to dry. This will make it much easier to string your beads!

2. Start off by stringing the small 1 cm (⅜ in) bead for your snake's nose and slide it to the center (i.e. half-way point) of your string. Then take both ends of the string and insert them through the hole in the bead designated as your snake's head. This will leave you with the string looped once through the nose and both ends of the string re-emerging from the same side of the snake's head. Make any adjustments to the beads so that the two halves of the strings emerging from the snake's head are the same length.

3. Set 2 beads aside, and slide both ends of the string through the rest of your beads, wheels and spools.

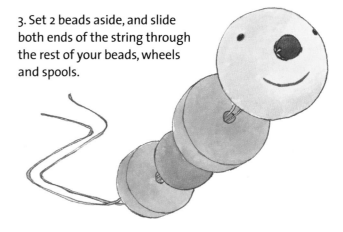

4. For the final bead of your snake, insert one piece of your string through a bead, and then slide this bead up to meet the rest of the snake's body. Next, using both halves of the string, tie a secure overhand knot right behind this final bead.

5. To keep both pieces of your string together, tie the two parts together at 9 cm (3½ in) intervals using overhand knots.

6. When you have approximately 9 cm (3½ in) left of string, insert one end of the string through an extra bead and pull the bead to meet the previous knot. Make an overhand knot using both ends of the string to secure the bead in place. This final bead will add a nice finishing touch to the pull-string of your snake.

7. The snakes I made have cheerful cerise noses and friendly smiles. They are hardly snake-like at all, and their happy smiles are irresistible...

Peg Doll Necklaces & Zipper-Pulls

SUPPLIES

4 cm (1⅝ in) boy-pegs

3 cm (1³⁄₁₆ in) tot or baby/bee shape pegs

Thin ribbon, colorful twine, or yarn

Sandpaper (optional)

Beeswax polish and a soft rag or paper toweling for application

A handheld drill and a 1 mm (¹⁄₁₆ in) drill bit

A woodworking vice and soft plastic vice jaw pads

13mm (US size 216½) screw eye rings

Watercolors (or paint of your choice) and brushes

Colored pencils

PVA or white craft glue

Glitter

Scissors

These necklaces and zipper-pulls are a fun way for children to take their peg doll friends with them wherever they go.

SMALL HELPING HANDS

- - - - - - - - - - - - - - - - - - -

As much as children love receiving dolls created by an adult, it's my experience that they love creating their own designs even more. For this project, an adult will need to drill a hole in the head of the peg doll and insert the screw eye, but after that, the doll can be handed over to be decorated. While the paint is drying, a child might enjoy choosing a colorful ribbon.

Preparing the doll

1. Secure one or two dolls at a time in a woodworking vice. Make a small pencil mark right at the top of the head of each doll, and drill ½ cm (¼ in) down.

2. Remove doll(s) from vice and insert screw eyes into the hole(s) at the tops of the heads.

Decorating the doll

1. Prior to painting, you may choose to give your doll a quick once-over with some sandpaper to smooth any rough portions (especially on the head of the doll where you plan to draw or paint a face).

2. Paint the hair and body of your doll. Add a face with paint or pencil. If you used watercolor paint, you can apply a small amount of beeswax polish to the hair and body if you wish. Note: *I don't recommend using polish on the face as it can cause the paint to smudge.*

3. Decorations made from felt and glued onto a doll may become damaged when the doll is worn. A fun option is to add touches of glitter. I painted little wings on the backs of some of my dolls. When the paint was dry, I used a paint brush to apply a thin layer of glue over the wings and then sprinkled on some glitter.

4. For a necklace, cut approximately 76 cm (30 in) of yarn, ribbon, or colorful twine, thread it through the screw eye, use an overhand knot to secure the ends and loop over the head of an eager child. For a zipper-pull, cut approximately 15 cm (6 in) ribbon or twine, thread it through the screw eye. Then loop the thread through the end of the zipper pull-tag and secure to desired length with an overhand knot. Use scissors to trim ends of excess ribbon or twine.

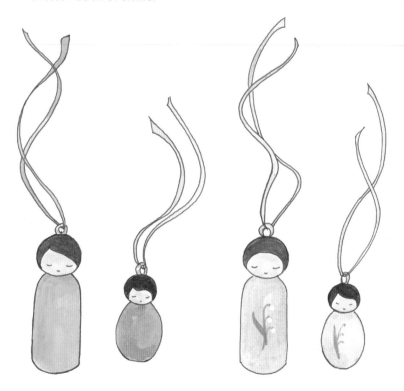

Holiday Ornaments

SUPPLIES

5 cm (2 in) angel-pegs

4 cm (1 ⅝ in) boy-pegs

White and red wool felt (or other colors of your choice)

Tracing paper or a photocopy of patterns

Needle and embroidery floss

Thin ribbon, twine, or thread

A bit of brown yarn for hair

Silver pipe-cleaner wire

Sandpaper (optional)

A handheld drill and a 1 mm (¹⁄₁₆ in) drill bit

A woodworking vice and soft plastic vice jaw pads

13mm (US size 216½) screw eye rings

Watercolors (or paint of your choice) and brushes

White acrylic paint

Beeswax polish and a soft rag or paper toweling for application

Colored pencils

PVA or white craft glue

Fabric scissors

Glitter

O Tannenbaum, o Tannenbaum,
wie treu sind deine Blätter!
Du grünst nicht nur zur Sommerzeit,
Nein auch im Winter, wenn es schneit.
O Tannenbaum, o Tannenbaum,
wie treu sind deine Blätter!

O Tannenbaum, o Tannenbaum!
Du kannst mir sehr gefallen!
Wie oft hat nicht zur Weihnachtszeit
Ein Baum von dir mich hoch erfreut!
O Tannenbaum, o Tannenbaum!
Du kannst mir sehr gefallen!

O Tannenbaum, o Tannenbaum!
Dein Kleid will mich was lehren:
Die Hoffnung und Beständigkeit
Gibt Trost und Kraft zu jeder Zeit.
O Tannenbaum, o Tannenbaum!
Das soll dein Kleid mich lehren.

SMALL HELPING HANDS

- - - - - - - - - - - - - - - - - -

Children love creating gifts for others and also being able to add their own handmade decorations to the home. For this project, an adult will need to drill a hole in the head of the peg doll and insert the screw eye, but after that, the doll can be handed over to be decorated. Children will also enjoy choosing the ribbon or string from which their ornaments can hang.

Preparing the doll

1. Secure one or two dolls at a time in a woodworking vice. Make a small pencil mark right at the top of the head of each doll, and drill ½cm (¼in) down.

2. Remove doll(s) from vice and insert screw eyes into the holes at the tops of the heads.

Decorating an angel

1. Prior to painting, you may choose to give your angel a quick once-over with some sandpaper to smooth any rough portions (especially on the head where you plan to draw or paint a face).

2. Paint the hair and body of your angel. I painted the bodies of my angels white; however, you might choose some other color. Be sure that the color you use to paint the body of your doll matches the color of your glitter! Add a face with paint or pencil.

3. Pour a small amount of glue into a disposable cup, add a drop of water, mix with a paint brush and then use the paintbrush to lightly coat the body of your angel with the diluted glue. Working over a clean piece of paper to catch excess glitter, sprinkle glitter over the body.

4. Cut out wings from felt according to the pattern and attach to the back to your angel with a bit of glue.

Angel wings

5. Cut approximately 7cm (2⅝ in) of silver pipe-cleaner wire, twist into a small circle and use a bit of glue to secure to the head of your angel.

6. Cut approximately 15 cm (6 in) of ribbon, twine, or thread, string it through the screw eye, and secure to desired length with an overhand knot. Use scissors to trim ends.

Decorating a gnome

1. Prior to painting, you may choose to give your gnome a quick once-over with some sandpaper to smooth any rough portions (especially on the head of the gnome where you plan to draw or paint a face).

2. Paint the hair and body of your gnome, and add a face with paint or pencil.

3. If you used watercolor paint, you can apply a small amount of beeswax polish to the hair and body if you wish. Note: *I don't recommend using polish on the face as it can cause the paint to smudge.*

Gnome hat

4. Cut out a gnome hat according to the pattern. Overlap the two straight sides, adjust to fit the head of the doll and, using a flat appliqué stitch, sew to form a cone shape. Attach to the head of your doll with a small amount of glue. If you would like to add plaits to your mama gnome, prepare them from a bit of yarn and glue them in place prior to gluing her hat.

5. For papa-gnome's beard, needle felt a few wisps of wool roving, trim and glue to the chin of your doll. If you don't have wool roving, you can glue on some small pieces of wool yarn.

6. When all the glue has dried and the hat is secure, prepare a needle with thread. Run the needle through the hat and secure to desired length with an overhand knot. Use scissors to trim ends.

Cake Toppers for Birthdays, Weddings & other Celebrations

Who doesn't love cake? We eat it as often as possible in my house. A birthday? Time for cake! Grandparents are visiting? Time for cake! It's Tuesday? Time for cake! These little cupcake decorations can be customized for any festive occasion, and for extra fun you can customize hair color and costume décor accordingly.

SMALL HELPING HANDS

- - - - - - - - - - - - - - - - - -

The job of using a saw to cut the dowel is best left to an adult; however, children will certainly enjoy painting their own cupcake decorations!

SUPPLIES

5 cm (2 in) angel-pegs

4 cm (1⅝ in) boy-pegs

Wooden oval or disc, at least 7.5 cm (3 in) wide for wedding topper

Wooden wheel, 3.5 cm (1½ in) wide with 6 mm (¼ in) hole for cupcake topper

Wooden dowel, 6 mm (¼ in) diameter for cupcake topper

Yellow, white, light blue, gray and black wool felt (or other colors of your choice)

White tulle (for brides)

A small bit of yarn for hair and/or a beard

Tracing paper or a photocopy of patterns

Needle and white thread

Embroidery floss: gray and green

Sandpaper (optional)

A small saw suitable for cutting wood

A woodworking vice and soft plastic vice jaw pads

A pencil sharpener

Watercolors (or paint of your choice) and brushes

White acrylic paint (optional)

Beeswax polish and a soft rag or paper toweling for application

Colored pencils

PVA or white craft glue

Cellophane tape

Lily-of-the-Valley millinery stems: see resource guide for purchasing information

Fabric scissors

Constructing the base for cupcake toppers

1. Using your pencil sharpener, sharpen one end of a dowel.

2. Measure approximately 5 cm (2 in) from the pointed tip of your dowel and mark with a pencil.

3. Secure your dowel in a woodworking vice and use a saw to cut the dowel at the pencil mark. Use sandpaper to smooth any jagged edges left by the saw.

4. Insert the flat end of the dowel into the center of your wooden wheel. If the dowel is too big for the hole, use sandpaper to gradually sand down the diameter of your dowel until it can be inserted into the hole. Do not sand it down too much – the dowel should fit tightly.

5. Add a little bit of wood glue inside the hole of the wheel and insert the flat end of your piece of dowel. The flat end should sit 1 mm (1/16 in) below, or flush with the top edge of the wheel. You must ensure that the flat end does not project above the top of the wheel at all. Be sure to push it down.

6. Paint the wheel-portion of the base using non-toxic acrylic paint, non-toxic watercolors or leave the wood of the base unfinished. If you have used watercolor paint on your base, rub with a small amount of beeswax polish to remove excess paint and seal the wood.

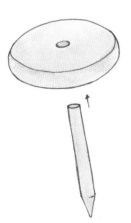

Birthday figure cupcake topper

1. Prior to painting, you may choose to give your doll a quick once-over with some sandpaper to smooth any rough portions (especially on the head of the doll where you plan to draw or paint a face).

2. Paint the hair and body of your doll. Add a face with paint or pencil. If you use watercolor paint, you can apply a small amount of beeswax polish to the hair and body if you wish. Note: *I don't recommend using polish on the face as it can cause the paint to smudge.*

3. To create plaits, prepare a braided length from a bit of yarn and glue it over the top of the head with the ends hanging down.

Crown

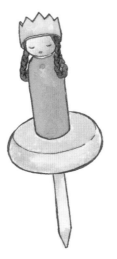

4. To create the crown, use pinking shears to cut a 6 cm (2¼ in) length of wool felt and glue carefully in place around the head of your doll.

5. Glue figure to the center of the base and allow glue to dry.

Bunny figure for cupcake topper

1. Prior to painting, you may choose to give your doll a quick once-over with some sandpaper to smooth any rough portions (especially on the head of the doll where you plan to draw or paint a face).

2. Paint the head and body of your doll, leaving a circle or oval space for the face. Add facial features with paint or pencil. If you use watercolor paint, you can apply a small amount of beeswax polish to the painted areas if you wish. Note: *I don't recommend using polish on the face as it can cause the paint to smudge.*

3. Cut out bunny ears from felt according to pattern and use a small bit of glue to secure to the back of the head.

Bunny ears

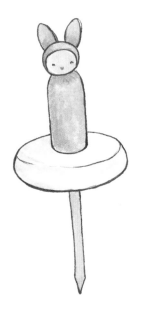

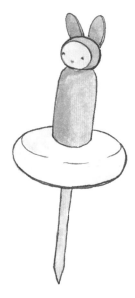

4. Glue figure to center of the base and allow glue to dry.

Note: *To clean the cupcake and cake toppers, wipe the base with a damp rag and allow to dry. You may even run the dowel portion of the cupcake toppers under water, but take care to avoid immersing the peg doll figures in water.*

WEDDING CAKE TOPPERS

This day, my Julia, thou must make
For Mistress Bride the wedding-cake:
Knead but the dough, and it will be
To paste of almonds turn'd by thee;
Or kiss it thou but once or twice,
And for the bride-cake there'll be spice.

Robert Herrick

Decorating the bride

1. Prior to painting, you may choose to give your doll a quick once-over with some sandpaper to smooth any rough portions (especially on the head of the doll where you plan to draw or paint a face).

2. Paint the hair of your doll and add a face with paint or pencil. For fun, you can customize the hair color to match the recipient of the cake topper. There is no need to apply paint to the body of your bride because it will be covered with felt. If, however, you wish to create a shorter dress with a visible underskirt (as I did for one of my dolls), then paint the bottom third of the doll's body whatever color you choose.

3. Choose a dress pattern and cut out from felt according to the pattern. For fun, you might consider customizing the bridal gown to match the wedding dress of the bride for whom this cake topper is intended. If you would like your bride to carry a bouquet of flowers, use green thread to stitch the flowers to the front of the dress. After the bouquet is sewn on the front, glue the dress around the body of your doll and sew up the back with a few stitches of white thread.

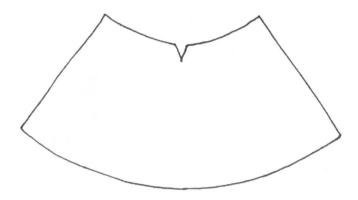

Bridal dress A

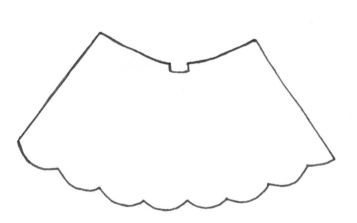

Bridal dress B

4. For the veil, cut a piece of tulle approximately 5.5 cm (2 ¼ in) by 8 cm (8 ⅛ in) and a small oval of white felt approximately 2 cm (¾ in) wide. Using white thread, sew a running stitch across the wide edge of the tulle and then tack the tulle with a few stitches onto the circle of white felt. You can also stitch the stems of tiny millinery flowers to the felt circle. Glue the veil to the back of the doll's head and trim the end of the veil if it seems too long.

Bridal veil head piece

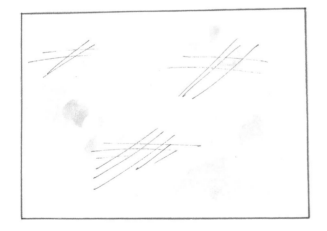

Tulle bridal veil

Decorating the groom

1. Prior to painting, you may choose to give your doll a quick once-over with some sandpaper to smooth any rough portions (especially on the head of the doll where you plan to draw or paint a face).

2. Paint the hair and add a face with paint or pencil. You can paint the hair color to match the groom for whom the cake topper is intended, and add other distinguishing features such as a beard or glasses. Note: *Glasses can be drawn in with pencil and a beard can be made from a bit of yarn or wisp of wool roving.*

3. Paint the top half of the body white and the bottom half of the body gray.

4. Choose a jacket pattern for your groom (either a standard suit jacket or a morning coat with tails) and cut out from black felt according to the pattern. Add French knot buttons and glue the jacket onto the doll with the front overlapping and the buttons on top.

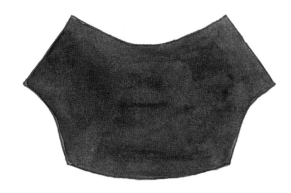

Groom long morning coat

Groom suit jacket

5. Choose a tie design (either standard or bow tie), cut out felt according to the pattern and glue to the doll. Note: *If you choose a standard tie, you will want to tuck the tip beneath the front of the jacket.*

6. To make the top hat, cut out pieces of felt according to the patterns. Sew piece A into a cylinder and stitch piece B to the top. Using tiny stitches, attach the other end of the cylinder to the brim of the hat (piece C). Sew or glue on a contrasting hat band and then attach the hat to the head of your doll with glue.

Standard tie   Bow tie

Top hat side A

Top hat brim C   Top hat top B

Preparing the base for the wedding cake topper

1. Paint the top and side edges of a wooden oval or disc.

2. If you would like to add a flowered arch, take 2 wired stems of millinery flowers. The ones I used are 15 cm (6 in) long. Measure 4 cm (1½ in) at the ends of the wires and create a right-angle bend in each. Using cellophane tape, secure the bent wire sections underneath the wooden disc – one stem of flowers to each side of the disc. Then curve the flowers to meet in an arc over the center of the disc. (I tried several ways to attach flowered arches to the bases of my wedding cake toppers, and the least elegant, but simplest method was, indeed, to use cellophane tape!)

3. Glue dolls in place on the base.

Part Two

Toys that Spin & Fly

Spinning Tops & Dreidels

In our house, spinning tops are some of the most played with toys, and when Hanukkah rolls around, our dreidel collection comes out of the cupboard to join our usual favorites. Traditional dreidels have four sides, with a Hebrew letter painted on each of

SUPPLIES

3 cm (1³⁄₁₆ in) tot or baby/bee-shaped pegs

4.8 cm (1⁷⁄₈ in) wooden wheels with 0.6 cm (¼ in) center holes

Tulle or other fabric for skirt

Tracing paper or a photocopy of skirt pattern

Needle and matching thread

6 mm (¼ in) diameter dowels (or dowels with diameter matching the center holes of your wheels)

Small saw suitable for cutting wood

Woodworking vice

Watercolors (or paint of your choice) and brushes

Beeswax polish and a soft rag or paper toweling for application

A pencil sharpener

Sandpaper

Wood glue (or other strong craft glue)

Colored pencils

Fabric scissors

the four surfaces. The letters are '*nun*,' '*gimmel*,' '*hay*,' and '*shin*,' standing for the Hebrew phrase, '*Nes Gadol Hayah Sham*' (A Great Miracle Happened There). The phrase refers to the story surrounding the relighting of the menorah within the temple in Jerusalem after its destruction in 168 BCE, and this proper sort of dreidel with four sides is required for playing the traditional Hanukkah game. We also own several dreidels which are fun to spin, but are not particularly functional – these dreidels have all the letters, but don't have four sides! Still, they serve as a reminder of the story of Hanukkah and its beautiful theme of bringing forth light from places of darkness.

I have designed these little tops with peg dolls in place of the spindles, and to several I have added the four Hebrew letters symbolic of the traditional Hanukkah game. To these special Hanukkah tops I also added silver coin-shaped dots to represent the tokens used when playing a game of dreidel. But painted any bright color, these sweet spinning tops make perfect gifts or party favors. I hope you enjoy painting them up and giving them a spin as much we enjoy them in our house, too!

SMALL HELPING HANDS
- - - - - - - - - - - - - - - - - -

While the job of using a saw to cut the dowel is best left to an adult, children of any age will enjoy painting these tops.

Constructing the top

1. Using your pencil sharpener, sharpen one end of a dowel.

2. Insert the pointed end of the dowel into the center of your wooden wheel. If the dowel is too big for the hole, use your sandpaper to gradually sand down the diameter of your dowel until it can be inserted into the hole. Do not sand it down too much – the dowel should still fit tightly.

2. Measure approximately 2.5 cm (1 in) from the pointed tip of your dowel and mark with a pencil.

3. Secure your dowel in a woodworking vice and use your saw to cut the dowel at the pencil mark. Use sandpaper to smooth away any jagged edges.

4. Add a little bit of wood glue inside the hole of the wheel and insert the flat end of your tiny piece of dowel. The flat end should sit 1 mm (1/16 in) below, or flush with the top edge of the wheel. You must ensure that the flat end does not project above the top of the wheel at all. Be sure to push it down.

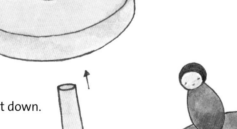

5. Paint and decorate the top however you wish. If you have used watercolor paint you can rub with a small amount of beeswax polish to seal the wood.

Decorating the doll

1. Prior to painting, you may choose to give your doll a quick once-over with some sandpaper to smooth any rough portions (especially on the head of the doll where you plan to draw or paint a face).

2. Paint the hair and body of your doll. Add a face with paint or pencil. If you used watercolor paint, you can apply a small amount of beeswax polish to the hair and body if you wish. Note: *I don't recommend using polish on the face as it can cause the paint to smudge.*

Finishing the top

1. Glue the base of the doll to the center of the top.

2. If you want to add a skirt, use the pattern to cut your tulle or other fabric. With a needle and thread, create a running stitch around the center circle. Place the skirt around the base of your doll, pull tight to gather the fabric and secure end of thread.

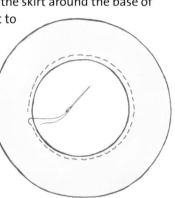

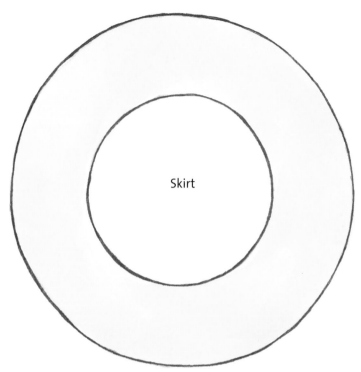

Skirt

A Butterfly Garden Mobile

SUPPLIES

Seven 5 cm (2 in) angel-pegs

An embroidery hoop, approximately 23 cm (9 in) in diameter

A few tones of wool felt (I used tones of yellow and orange – you might choose other colors)

Origami or colorful scrapbook paper (optional)

Tracing paper or a photocopy of patterns

Watercolors (or paint of your choice) and brushes

PVA or other white craft glue

Sandpaper (optional)

Beeswax polish and a soft rag or paper toweling for application

A handheld drill and a 1 mm (1/16 in) drill bit

A woodworking vice and soft plastic vice jaw pads

13mm (US size 216½) screw eye rings

White heavyweight button thread

Embroidery floss in various colors

Millinery flower stamens

6 small beads

Paintbrushes

Pencils

Fabric scissors

I've watched you now a full half-hour;
Self-poised upon that yellow flower
And, little Butterfly! indeed
I know not if you sleep or feed.
How motionless! – not frozen seas
More motionless! and then
What joy awaits you, when the breeze
Hath found you out among the trees,
And calls you forth again!

William Wordsworth

SMALL HELPING HANDS

- - - - - - - - - - - - - - - - - - -

For this project, a small child might like to help pick the color scheme, sand the peg dolls and paint the embroidery hoop from which the butterflies will be suspended. Slightly older children could create the butterflies on their own; however, they should have adult assistance using the drill, and they might also need help stringing the mobile.

Preparing the dolls

1. Secure one or two dolls at a time in a woodworking vice. Make a small pencil mark on the back of each doll, ½ cm (¼ in) down from where the head meets the body and drill ½ cm (¼ in) deep.

2. Remove doll(s) from vice and insert screw eyes into the holes.

Butterfly wings

Antenna holder

Fold antenna

Decorating the dolls

1. Prior to painting, you may choose to give your dolls a quick once-over with some sandpaper to smooth any rough portions (especially on the heads of the dolls where you plan to draw or paint a face).

2. Paint the hair and body of your dolls. Add faces with paint or pencil. If you use watercolor paint, you can apply a small amount of beeswax polish to the hair and bodies if you wish. Note: *I don't recommend using polish on the faces as it can cause the paint to smudge.*

3. To hold the butterfly antennae in place, cut seven small circles of felt 1.2 cm (½ in) in diameter. Bend a millinery flower stamen in half, put a small amount of glue on one of the felt circles, set the bent section of the stamen into the dot of glue and then apply to the back of the head of a doll. Repeat for all the butterflies. Note: *If you do not have millinery flower stamens, you can use short lengths of heavyweight button thread for antennae.*

4. Cut out wings according to the pattern for each of your butterflies. Creating wings from colorful craft paper is a fun option (see above for inspiration) or you can make the wings, as I did, from soft tones of felt. Once the wings are cut out, glue them in place just under the screw eyes on the backs of the dolls.

Constructing the mobile

1. Paint the embroidery hoop.

2. To create the hanging flowers, cut 4 leaf shapes (A), 4 large flower shapes (B), one medium flower shape (C), and one small flower shape (D). Cut a slit in each flower/leaf where indicated by dotted line(s) on the pattern. Overlap one full petal on each flower to form shallow cones and stitch to hold the shape. For the leaf shapes, overlap 0.5 cm (¼ in) at each cut and stitch in place.

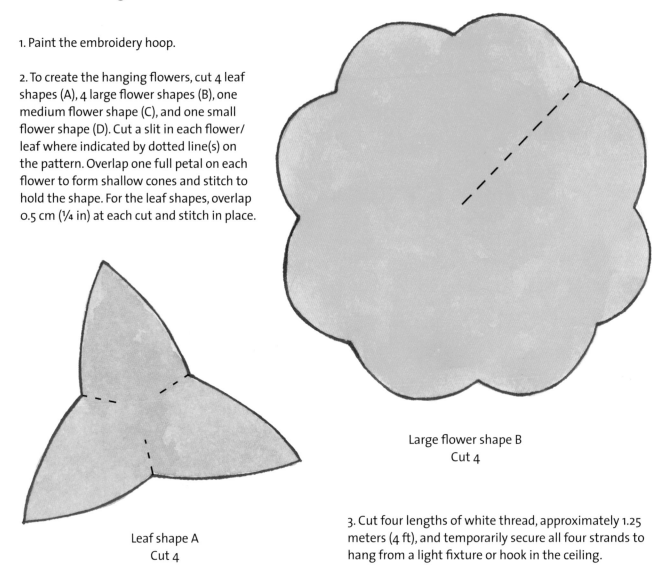

Large flower shape B
Cut 4

Leaf shape A
Cut 4

3. Cut four lengths of white thread, approximately 1.25 meters (4 ft), and temporarily secure all four strands to hang from a light fixture or hook in the ceiling.

Medium flower shape C
Cut 1

Small flower shape D
Cut 1

4. Measure 80 cm (30 in) down. Secure one of the threads around the embroidery hoop with a double knot, allowing the remaining portion of string to hang down (later this will be used for hanging a butterfly). Measure a third of the way around the hoop and knot a second thread at the same height. Measure a third of the way around again, and knot a third thread, allowing the fourth thread to hang down through the center of the hoop. Suspended from three points, the hoop will hang horizontally.

5. Untie or unhook the tops of the threads from the ceiling hook/light fixture. While holding the threads together in one hand, lay the hoop flat on a table. With the hoop lying level on the table, measure approximately 20–25 cm (8–10 in) up from the hoop and knot all four strands together. Now, temporarily secure the tops of the four strands once again to the light fixture or ceiling hook so you can finish stringing the mobile.

6. Thread a needle onto the fourth thread (the one which is hanging through the center of the hoop). Run the needle down through the center of one of the leaf shapes (pattern piece A) and then down through the center of one of the large flower shapes (pattern piece B). Push them up the string and out of your way, and then thread a bead onto the string. Secure the bead with a single knot at a height even with the embroidery hoop, then slide the flower and leaf to rest on top of the bead. Run the needle down through the center of the medium flower shape (pattern piece B) and then secure a bead with a single knot approximately 2.5 cm (1 in) down from the flower above. Repeat with the smallest flower shape (pattern piece A). The single knots will allow you to slide the beads and adjust the heights of the flowers. Once all three flowers are secured, you can adjust their heights according to your preference.

7. Refer to earlier instructions for securing leaves and large flower shapes to the three strings hanging from the embroidery hoop.

8. Next, cut three pieces of thread, 46 cm (18 in) each. Tie the threads to the embroidery hoop, one between each of the strings securing the hoop. You should now have 6 threads hanging down from the hoop, plus the one in the center. Hang a butterfly peg doll from each thread. My butterflies are hanging at different lengths, some at 14 cm (5 ½ in) and some at 18 cm (7 in) down from the hoop. You can secure your butterflies at various heights according to your preference.

9. Once you have made adjustments and are satisfied with how your mobile is hanging, use scissors to clip the extra ends of thread.

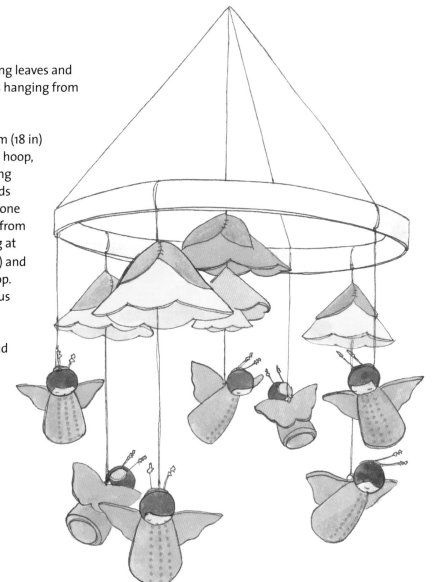

A Forest of Fireflies Mobile & Rod Puppets

SUPPLIES

Six 5 cm (2 in) angel-pegs

A small tree branch, approximately 51 cm (20 in) in length

Wool felt, red and black

White tulle

Green wax kite-paper (or other type of green paper)

Tracing paper or a photocopy of patterns

Watercolors (or paint of your choice) and brushes

Glow-in-the-dark paint

PVA or other white craft glue

Sandpaper (optional)

Beeswax polish and a soft rag or paper toweling for application

A handheld drill and a 1 mm (¹⁄₁₆ in) drill bit

A woodworking vice and soft plastic vice jaw pads

13 mm (US size 216½) screw eye rings

Beige heavyweight button thread

Red & black embroidery floss

Black millinery flower stamens (or black button thread)

Pencils

Fabric scissors

To a Firefly

Stars are twinkling up on high,
Moon hangs low in eastern sky;
These with thee do not compare,
Cheerful beacon of the air –

Speeding onward through the dark,
Beneath the oak trees in the park,
With thy glowing, gleaming light,
Happy lightning bug of night.

Sir John Morris-Jones

I love how the fireflies on this mobile seem to flit beneath the branches of leafy summer trees, and when the lights go out, the tail-ends of these little firefly peg dolls will glow in the dark!

SMALL HELPING HANDS
- - - - - - - - - - - - - - - - - -

Young children would have fun exploring outside to help find a nice branch for this project, and they could also assist by removing the leaves from the branch. Applying the black and yellow paint on the dolls for this project can be tricky, but once the colors are dry, the task of adding glow-in-the-dark paint is a fun job for small hands!

Preparing the dolls

1. Secure one or two dolls at a time in a woodworking vice. Make a small pencil mark on the back of each doll, ½ cm (¼ in) down from where the head meets the body and drill ½ cm (¼ in) deep.

2. Remove doll(s) from vice and insert screw eyes into the holes.

Decorating the dolls

1. Prior to painting, you may choose to give your dolls a quick once-over with some sandpaper to smooth any rough portions (especially on the heads of the dolls where you plan to draw or paint a face).

2. Using a pencil, draw around the bodies of your dolls to indicate the bottom third. Cover the heads and upper two-thirds of the bodies with black paint, leaving unpainted ovals for the faces. Add faces with paint or pencil. If you use watercolor paint, you can apply a small amount of beeswax polish over the black paint. Note: *The dark pigment of black watercolor paint, can be especially messy when waxed. Please be very careful to avoid transferring paint residue onto the faces or unpainted lower portion of the dolls.*

3. Paint the bottom third of the bodies a bright yellow color. Allow to dry, and then paint over it with glow-in-the-dark paint. I found it was best to add five or six coats of glow-in-the-dark to get a good glowing effect. Luckily, this paint will dry quickly; by the time you have painted a layer of glow-in-the-dark on all six dolls, the paint on first one will be dry and you can start applying the next layer.

4. Cut out the red capes and 2 black wing-covers from felt, plus the white tulle under-wings for each of your fireflies according to the patterns. Clip ½ cm (¼ in) down (as per the dotted line on the pattern) at the center of each red cape (this will accommodate the screw eye at the back of each doll.)

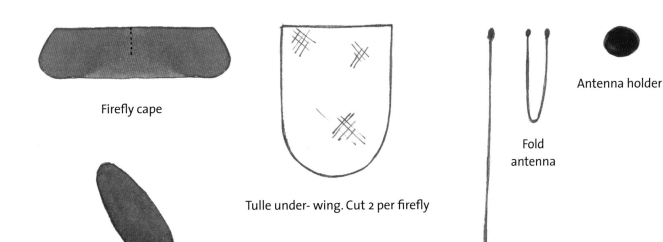

Firefly cape

Tulle under- wing. Cut 2 per firefly

Fold antenna

Antenna holder

Firefly wing. Cut 2 per firefly

5. Apply a thin line of glue along the length of the red cape and affix around the shoulders of a doll (the screw eye should fit neatly into the slit you have cut in the cape). To secure the front of the cape, stitch with red embroidery floss.

6. For the wings, thread a needle with black embroidery floss or thread, use a running stitch to gather the top of a tulle wing, sew the gathered edge of the tulle wing down to one end of a black felt wing-cover, and then sew to the back of the red cape with the white tulle beneath the black wing-cover. Repeat for all wings.

7. To hold the firefly antennae in place, cut six small ovals of black felt 1.2 cm (½ in) wide. Bend a black millinery flower stamen in half, put a small amount of glue on one of the felt ovals, set the bent section of the stamen into the dot of glue and then apply to the back of the head of a doll. Repeat for all the fireflies.
Note: *If you do not have black millinery flower stamens, you can use short lengths of black heavyweight button thread for antennae.*

Constructing the mobile

1. Cut two lengths of beige button thread approximately 61 cm (24 in) each, and six lengths of beige button thread approximately 38 cm (15 in) each.

2. Cut 25 small leaves from green wax kite paper (or other green paper).

3. Using one of the 61 cm (24 in) threads, knot ends to each end of the tree branch. Knot the other long thread to the center of the thread you have just tied to the branch. Use this thread to hang your mobile from a hook or light fixture. Note: *You can slide this hanging-thread to adjust the balance of the tree branch.*

4. Tie the shorter lengths of thread, one to each of your six fireflies. Then, for each firefly, attach a needle to the thread, sew a stitch through one or two paper leaves and tie the firefly to a spot on the tree branch. Adjust the paper leaves to pleasing heights along the threads.

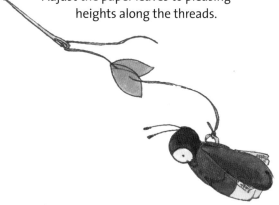

5. Once all 6 fireflies are tied to the branch, you can decorate the branch with the remaining paper leaves. To do this, squeeze a small amount of glue into a small, disposable container, lightly dip the tip of each paper leaf in the glue and place the leaves in position on the branch.

A FIREFLY ROD PUPPET

This is a wonderful project to encourage active play. What fun to take these little rod puppets in hand and go flitting among the trees together!

Preparing the dolls

1. Secure one or two dolls at a time in a woodworking vice with the heads facing down. Using a 6 mm (¼ in) drill bit, drill a hole in the base(s) approximately 1.5 cm (⁷⁄₁₆ in) deep.

2. Use a small saw to cut 6 mm (¼ in) diameter dowel(s) to a length of approximately 28 cm (11 in). Smooth the cut end with sandpaper.

Decorating the dolls

See doll making instructions for the firefly mobile (pages 72–73). Once the doll is finished, put a drop of wood glue into the hole in the base of the doll and insert one end of the cut dowel.

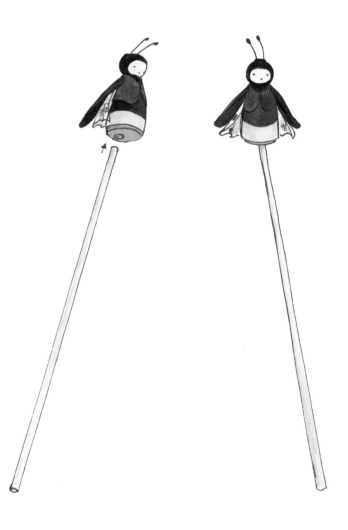

A Flying Bird Marionette

'Cold winter is coming,' said the swallow, 'and I am going to fly away into warmer countries. Will you go with me? You can sit on my back and fasten yourself on with your sash. Then we can fly far away over the mountains, where the sun shines more brightly than here; where it is always summer and the flowers bloom in greater beauty. Fly now with me, dear Thumbellina.'
'Yes, I will go with you,' said Thumbellina. And she seated herself on the bird's back with her feet on his outstretched wings, and tied her sash to one of his strongest feathers. Then the swallow rose in the air and flew over the forest and over sea, high above the highest mountains, covered with eternal snow...

From *Thumbellina* by Hans Christian Andersen

My favorite moment in the story of *Thumbellina* is when she escapes marriage to a disagreeable mole by flying away on the back of a swallow. The image of a tiny girl soaring over the mountains on the back of a bird has always stayed with me, and so I created this project...

When the bird is attached to strings like a marionette, it is capable of dramatic flight; however, I have designed the strings so that they can be easily detached. With the strings removed, this project makes a beautiful soft toy.

SMALL HELPING HANDS

- - - - - - - - - - - - - - - - - - -

A small child could help add stuffing to this little bird, and a novice at sewing could try his or her hand at stitching together layers for the wings and tail by substituting a whip stitch or running stitch for the more complicated blanket stitch. Of course, once the bird is completed, this little fellow will be happy to give rides to peg dolls created by hands both young and old.

SUPPLIES

Wool felt: dark blue, red and white (or whatever colors you choose for your bird)

Tracing paper or a photocopy of patterns

A small amount of stuffing

Embroidery floss to match your felt, plus black for the eye

Sewing needles

Watercolors (or paint of your choice) and brushes

Beeswax polish and a soft rag or paper toweling for application

A handheld drill and a 1 mm (¹⁄₁₆ in) drill bit

A woodworking vice and soft plastic vice jaw pads

Two flat craft sticks

Heavyweight button thread

Hook & eye fasteners (small: size 1 or 2)

Sandpaper (optional)

PVA or wood glue

Fabric scissors

Making the bird

1. Cut out all pieces from felt: two body pieces, one stomach, one contrasting throat, four wings, two tails, and two pockets.

Bird pocket. Cut 2

Bird wing. Cut 4

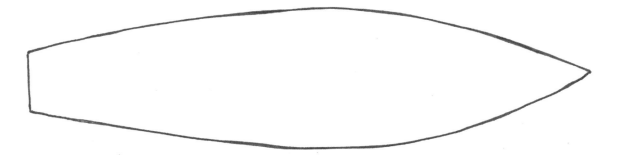

Bird stomach. Cut 1

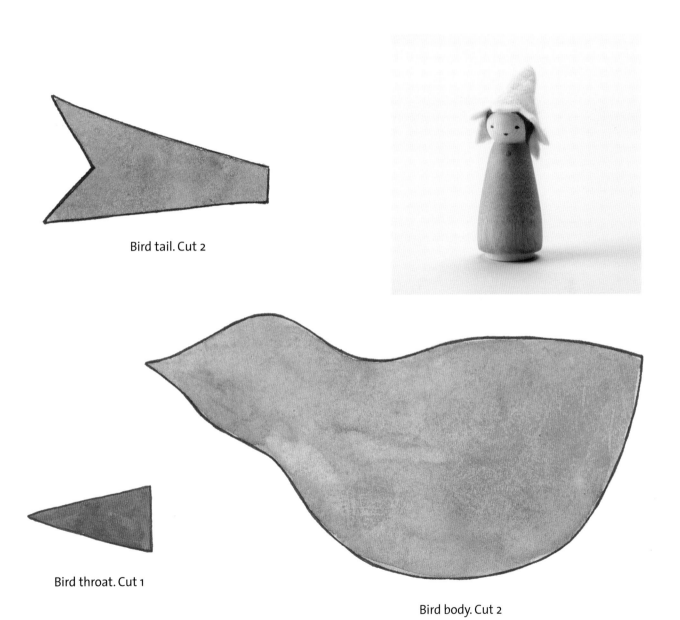

Bird tail. Cut 2

Bird throat. Cut 1

Bird body. Cut 2

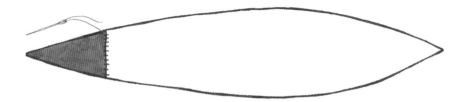

2. Overlap throat and stomach pieces ½ cm (¼ in). Using an appliqué stitch, stitch together.

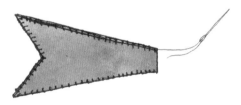

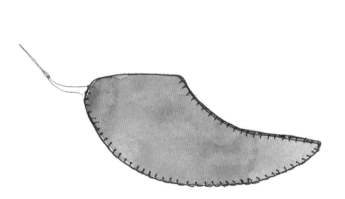

3. Put two wing pieces together and, using a blanket stitch, sew around the curved edges to form a double layer. Repeat for the second wing. Sew together the two tail pieces the same way.

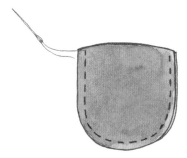

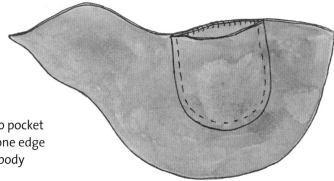

4. Use a running stitch to sew together the two pocket pieces, and then, with a blanket stitch, attach one edge of the pocket to the 'wrong side' of one of the body pieces (placement according to illustration).

5. Starting at the beak, use the blanket stitch to sew the two body pieces together along the back. When you come to the pocket, sew along the edge of the pocket which has not yet been attached, and then continue attaching the two body pieces along the back. Finish the seam when you arrive at the tail end.

6. Starting again at the beak, stitch the throat and stomach to one of the main body pieces. End the seam at the tail.

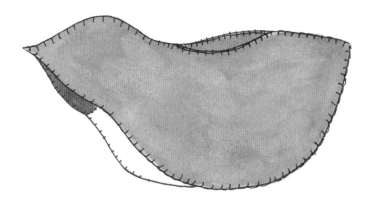

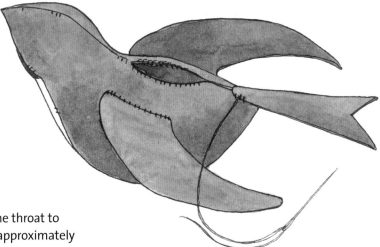

7. Return to the beak and start stitching the throat to the other side of the body. When you get approximately a third of the way along, stuff the head and then continue sewing. Once you have stitched another third of the seam place a doll in the pocket and add a small amount of stuffing around the pocket. It is important to stuff this section lightly; if you stuff it too firmly, you will not be able to insert a doll. Finish stuffing the tail end of the bird, continue the seam and end at the tail.

8. Pin the wings to the sides of the body (you can move them around to decide where they look best). Then, using small stitches, sew the top layer of felt to the body. Once this is done, turn the bird over to stitch the bottom layer of the wing to the body. Repeat for the second wing.

9. To attach the tail, sew it overlapping the tail-end of the body approximately 2 cm (¾ in).

NOTE
The bird is designed to carry dolls made from 5 cm (2 in) angel-pegs or 4 cm (1⅝ in) boy-pegs.

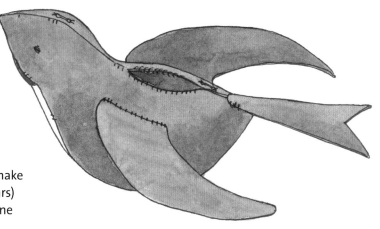

10. Using black embroidery floss, embroider an eye by adding French knots or a few straight stitches to either side of the head. Note: *You can hide your knots beneath one of the wings and run the thread through the body up to the head.*

11. If you would like to be able to attach strings to make your bird into a marionette, sew on the 'eyes' (or bars) for hook and eye fasteners – one at the head and one at the tail.

Assembling the 'T'

1. Drill small holes into either end of a flat craft stick. Using a second craft stick, glue it into a 'T'.

2. Cut two lengths of heavyweight button thread, approximately 38 cm (15 in) each. Tie one end of each thread through the holes in the craft stick. Knot the hook portions of the hook and eye fasteners to the other ends of the strings. Attach the hook fasteners to the eye portions on the bird, and now he can fly!

Decorating the doll

1. Prior to painting, you may choose to give your doll a quick once-over with some sandpaper to smooth any rough portions (especially on the head where you plan to draw or paint a face).

2. Paint the hair and body of your doll. Add a face with paint or pencil. If you used watercolor paint, you can apply a small amount of beeswax polish to the hair and body if you wish. Note: *I don't recommend using polish on the face as it can cause the paint to smudge.*

3. To make the gnome cap, cut out wool felt according to the pattern. Overlap the two straight sides, adjust to fit the head of the doll and, using a flat appliqué stitch, sew to form a cone shape. Attach the cap to the head of your doll with a small amount of glue.

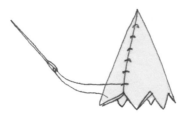

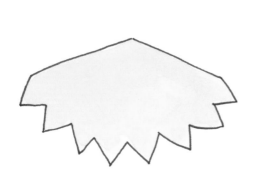

Gnome cap

A Dragon Rider Marionette

What child's imagination (or adult's imagination, for that matter) is not captured by the thought of riding on the back of a majestic dragon? Now you can create your own dragon and allow imaginations to soar!

SUPPLIES

5 cm (2 in) angel-peg or 4 cm (1⅝ in) boy-peg

Wool felt in three or four colors

Tracing paper or a photocopy of patterns

A small amount of stuffing

Embroidery floss to match your felt, plus black for the eye and nostril

Sewing needles

Watercolors (or paint of your choice) and brushes

Beeswax polish and a soft rag or paper toweling for application

A handheld drill and a 1 mm (1/16 in) drill bit

A woodworking vice and soft plastic vice jaw pads

Two flat craft sticks

Heavyweight button thread

Hook and eye fasteners (small: size 1 or 2)

Sandpaper (optional)

PVA or white craft glue

Fabric scissors

The dragon spread his shimmering wings and took off. Holding his breath, Ben clung tight to the spines of Firedrake's crest. The dragon rose higher and higher. They left the noise of the city behind. Night enfolded them in darkness and silence, and soon the human world was no more than a glitter of lights far below.

From *Dragon Rider* by Cornelia Funke

SMALL HELPING HANDS
- - - - - - - - - - - - - - - - - -

Choosing colors for my dragons was fun and interesting. Perhaps your child might like to help decide on the colors for her dragon? Children can also help add stuffing to the dragon's body, and a novice at sewing could try his or her hand at stitching together layers for the wings by substituting a whip stitch or running stitch for the more complicated blanket stitch. Once the dragon is completed, small hands can hold the wooden 'T' from which the dragon will hang while an adult adjusts the length of the strings. When the dragon's strings are firmly tied, it's time to take your peg dolls for a ride!

Making the dragon

1. Cut out all pieces from felt: two body pieces, one underbody, two ears, one back ridge, four wings, four front legs (two cut from tone A and two cut from tone B), four back legs (two from tone A and two from tone B), and two pockets.

Dragon front leg. Tone A cut 2

Dragon front leg. Tone B cut 2

Dragon back leg. Tone A cut 2

Dragon back leg. Tone B cut 2

Dragon body. Cut 2

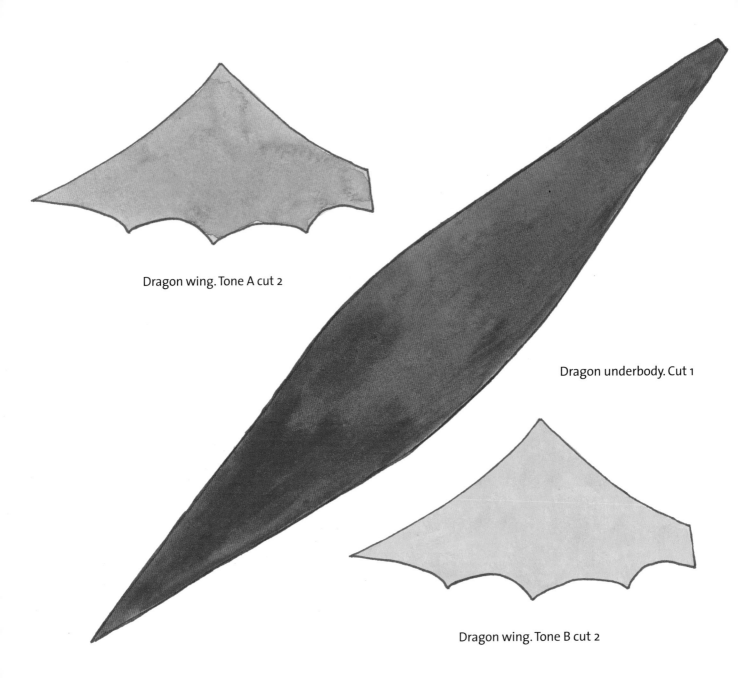

Dragon wing. Tone A cut 2

Dragon underbody. Cut 1

Dragon wing. Tone B cut 2

Dragon pocket. Cut 2

Dragon ear. Cut 2

Dragon back ridge. Cut 1

'All aboard!' said the dragon. 'Where shall we go?' 'We'll spend the night on the beach, and tomorrow we'll start on the long journey home. So, it's off to the shores of Tangerina!' shouted my father as the dragon soared above the dark jungle and the muddy river and all the animals bellowing at them and all the crocodiles licking pink lollipops and grinning wide grins.

From *My Father's Dragon* by Ruth Stiles Gannett

2. Use a running stitch to sew together the two pocket pieces, and then, also with a running stitch, attach one edge of the pocket to the wrong side of one of the body pieces (see illustration for placement of pocket).

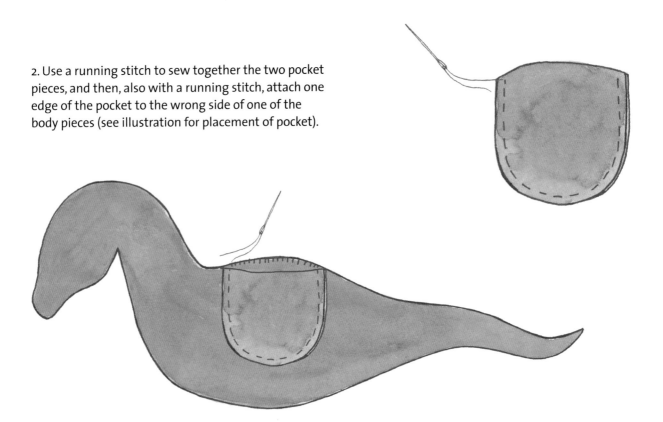

3. Sandwich the back ridge between the two body pieces so that it runs from the top of the head to the end of the tail. Pin these three sections (two body pieces and back ridge) in place.

4. Starting at the front of the snout, use the blanket stitch to sew the front part of the head together. When you get to the section where you have pinned the back ridge, use a running stitch through all three layers of felt. Be sure your stitches are small and even. When you come to the pocket, sew the edge of the pocket, back ridge and body together, then continue attaching the body pieces and back ridge. Finish the seam when you arrive at the tail end.

5. Starting again at the front of the snout, stitch the underbody beneath the head, down the neck and beneath the stomach. End the seam at the tail.

6. Return to the snout and start stitching the underbody to the other side of the head. Before you make the turn to stitch along the neck, stuff the head and then continue sewing. Once you have stitched another 5 cm (2 in), stuff the neck and then place a doll in the pocket. After you have sewn along the body beneath the pocket, add a small amount of stuffing around the pocket. It is important to stuff this section lightly; if you stuff it too firmly, you will not be able to insert a doll. Continue the seam and end at the tail.

7. Put two front leg pieces together (one of tone A and one of tone B). Attach the two layers of the claws with a small, even running stitch. Repeat this with the other front claw and the two back claws. NOTE: *Be sure that you have made one set of front and back legs for the RIGHT side of your dragon and the other set for the LEFT side of your dragon!*

8. Pin all four legs to the body (you can move them around a bit to decide on the best position). Sew the upper portions of the legs around the top layer of felt, allowing the contrasting color underneath to peek out along the side. This contrasting color will add a nice outline to the legs, giving them definition. Because the dragon is already stuffed, you may have to use larger stitches than you normally would to sew around the legs.

9. Put the two wing pieces together and, using a blanket stitch, sew around the edges to form a double layer. Repeat for the second wing.

10. Pin the wings to the sides of the body in your chosen position. Sew them firmly to the body.

11. Use a few stitches to attach the ears to either side of the head.

12. With black embroidery floss, embroider an eye by adding French knots or a few straight stitches to either side of the head, and with a contrasting embroidery floss, add nostrils to the end of the snout (you can hide the knots from the embroidery floss behind one of the ears).

13. If you would like to be able to attach strings to make your dragon into a marionette, sew on the 'eyes' (or bars) for hook and eye fasteners – one at the head and another closer to the tail.

Assembling the 'T'

1. Drill small holes into either end of a flat craft stick. Using a second craft stick, glue it into a 'T'.

2. Cut two lengths of heavyweight button thread, approximately 38 cm (15 in) each. Tie one end of each thread through the holes in the craft stick. Knot the hook portions of the hook and eye fasteners to the other ends of the strings. Attach the hook fasteners to the eye portions on the dragon so he can fly!

Decorating the doll

1. Prior to painting, you may choose to give your doll a quick once-over with some sandpaper to smooth any rough portions (especially on the head where you plan to draw or paint a face).

2. Paint the hair and body of your doll. Add a face with paint or pencil. If you used watercolor paint, you can apply a small amount of beeswax polish to the hair and body if you wish. Note: *I don't recommend using polish on the face as it can cause the paint to smudge.*

Part Three

Herbal Comforts & More Sewing Projects

Herbal Dream-Pillow & Peg Doll Dream-Companion

SUPPLIES

4 cm (1⅝ in) boy-peg (though any size doll will work)

¼ meter (¼ yard) natural color linen or other fabric of your choice

¼ meter (¼ yard) plain muslin or recycled pillow casing

2 colors of wool felt (I used blue and lavender)

Tracing paper or a photocopy of patterns

Sewing needles, matching thread, embroidery floss

A sewing machine (optional)

A small amount of unspun wool or other stuffing material

A handful of dried herbs: chamomile, rose petals, lavender, mint, cloves, rosemary, etc.

A small funnel with a 1.5 cm (⅝ in) opening or paper for creating a small funnel

Watercolors (or paint of your choice) and brushes

Fabric scissors

Sandpaper

Beeswax polish

This small, sweet-smelling cushion can be comforting to a child as he drifts off to sleep. Not only might the herbs inside the pillow help bring sweet dreams, but when the child wakes, he can confide his dreams to the tiny companion tucked into the star-pocket. This cushion could also double as a tooth fairy pillow – the pocket provides a safe place for a tooth, and it may also hold a small gift or coin left by the tooth fairy in exchange for the tooth.

When designing this project, I had a surplus of linen fabric. If you don't have any linen on hand, you could substitute any fabric you wish for the material of the pillow.

SMALL HELPING HANDS

- - - - - - - - - - - - - - - - -

A small child might enjoy painting his own dream-companion to sleep inside the pocket of this pillow or helping to stuff the pillow with wool and herbs, while a slightly older child might be able to help appliqué the star and sew on the pocket. For this, a child could use a running stitch, or whichever stitch he finds easiest.

Making the pillow

1. Cut two rectangles of linen (or other chosen fabric) for the exterior and two rectangles of muslin (or recycled pillow casing) for the interior lining according to the pattern.

Exterior pillow
Cut 2

Pillow lining
Cut 2

2. From wool felt, cut the star and pocket according to the patterns.

Star

Pocket

CHAMOMILE: Brings feelings of calm, and is said to keep bad dreams away
PEPPERMINT: Enhances clarity and vividness in dreams
ROSEMARY: Offers protection from bad dreams
ROSE PETALS: Brings feelings of warmth and love
LAVENDER: Is said to be soothing and relaxing
CLOVES: Brings warmth

3. Using an appliqué stitch, attach the star to the pocket and then stitch the pocket on three sides, slightly below center to one of the linen rectangles (see photograph on page 100 for placement).

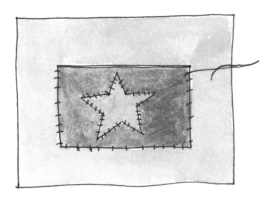

4. Create a stack of your rectangle pieces in the following fashion: First place the piece with the star-pocket facing up towards you, then lay the second linen rectangle over the piece with the pocket (if using fabric other than linen, lay the second rectangle face down), and finally, lay the two rectangles of muslin (or other fabric) over the two linen pieces. Pin in place and sew, by machine or hand, around the perimeter, leaving an unsewn opening of 7 cm (2½in) at the side or bottom.

5. Carefully clip extra fabric from the four corners of your cushion and then, via the unsewn section, turn your cushion right-side-out so the linen is on the outside and the muslin (or other fabric) layers are on the inside. Use a knitting needle or end of a paintbrush inside the corners to push them out so they are nicely shaped.

6. Use a funnel (or create a funnel from a cone of paper) to add a handful of dry herbs between the muslin lining layers. You could also carefully insert the herbs between the muslin layers using a teaspoon.

7. Add a small amount of wool (or other soft stuffing material) between the muslin and back layer of linen. Do not stuff firmly – the pillow will be more pleasing if it is stuffed softly.

8. Turn the edges in along the unsewn portion and use small stitches to close with matching thread.

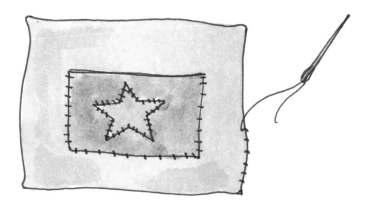

Decorating the doll

1. Prior to painting, you may choose to give your doll a quick once-over with some sandpaper to smooth any rough portions (especially on the head of the doll where you plan to draw or paint a face).

2. Paint the hair and body of your doll. You might paint the hair color to match the hair of the child who will be receiving the doll, and paint the body of the doll in his favorite color. For an extra touch of magic, a pair of fairy wings cut from wool felt could be glued to the back of the doll!

3. Add a face with paint or pencil.

4. If you used watercolor paint, you can apply a small amount of beeswax polish to the hair and body if you wish. Note: *I don't recommend using polish on the face as it can cause the paint to smudge.*

Autumn Lullaby

The sun has gone from the shining skies,
The dandelions have closed their eyes,
The stars are lighting their lamps to see
If babes and squirrels and birds and bees
Are sound asleep as they should be.

The squirrel keeps warm in his furs of gray,
'Neath feathers, birds are tucked away,
In yellow jackets, the bees sleep tight
And cuddle close through the chilly night,
My child is snug 'neath his blanket of white.

The squirrel nests in a big oak tree,
He finds a hole in the trunk, you see,
The robin's home is a nest overhead,
The bees, they nest in a hive instead,
My child's nest is his little bed.

Anonymous

A Rainbow of Herbal Comfort Friends

If all were rain and never sun,
No bow could span the hill;
If all were sun and never rain,
There'd be no rainbow still.

Christina Rossetti

SUPPLIES

2.5 cm (1 in) wooden bead

Two small wooden beads: 1 cm (³/₈ in) diameter

Wool felt in two pleasing colors (plus additional colors for small embellishments)

Pipe-cleaner wire (white or colored to match your felt)

Tracing paper or a photocopy of patterns

Matching embroidery floss and a needle

Star-shaped sequins (optional)

A handful of dried herbs: chamomile, rose petals, lavender, etc.

Several meters (yards) of sport weight wool yarn

3.25 mm (US size 3) knitting needles

PVA or other white craft glue

Watercolors (or paint of your choice) and brushes

Pencils

Fabric scissors

This poem by Christina Rossetti, with its message that we cannot have rainbows without rain, carries an underlying message that we cannot also have joy without some sadness. For me, as a parent, this is sometimes difficult, and I imagine it is difficult for other parents, too. We want to protect our children from every fear, anxiety and pain, but of course we cannot. However, we can do our best to support and guide our children to find the inner strength to move through difficulties. Perhaps these pocket-size dolls might be a tool to help this guiding process. In addition to the symbols these dolls wear, they are also stuffed with soothing herbs to delight not only the senses of touch and sight, but the sense of smell too. And they are sized perfectly to fit into a pocket so they can be carried through the day as a reminder of love.

SMALL HELPING HANDS

- - - - - - - - - - - - - - - - - -

A very young child could help choose the colors for this project and assist stuffing the doll with herbs. An older child might draw the face with a pencil and undertake the sewing; however, instead of the more complicated blanket stitch, a child might prefer to use a running stitch or whip stitch. For this project too, the help of small hands can add extra love and significance.

Knitting the hat

Gauge: 24 st to 10 cm (4 in)
Yarn: sport weight
Needle: 3.25 (US 3) or any needle to get gauge

Cast on 20 stitches
Row 1: Purl (and all odd rows: purl)
Row 2: Knit
Row 4: (k2, k2tog) Repeat to end of row (15 st)
Row 6: (k2, k2tog) x3, k3 st to end of row (12 st)
Row 8: (k2, k2tog) x3 (9 st)
Row 10: (k2, k2tog) twice, k1 (7 st)
Row 12: k2, k2tog, k3 (6 st)
Row 14: k2, k2tog, k2 (5 st)
Row 16: k2, k2tog, k1 (4 st)
Row 18: k1, k2tog, k1 (3 st)
Row 19: p2tog, p1 (2 st)

Cut the yarn leaving a tail, thread a darning needle and run through 2 stitches to fasten. Use the long tail to seam the hat into a cone shape and weave in ends.

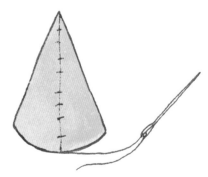

In case you are not a knitter, here is a pattern for a hat sewn from felt:

1. Using the pattern provided, cut one piece of wool felt to size.

2. Overlap the two straight sides, adjust to fit the head of the doll and, using a flat appliqué stitch, sew to form a cone shape. Attach to the head of your doll with glue.

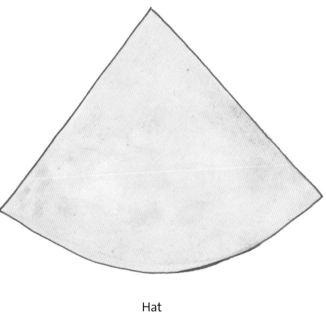

Hat

Stitching the appliqué emblems

HEART

1. Use patterns to cut a circle from pink felt and a heart from red (or other contrasting color) felt.

2. With an appliqué stitch, attach the heart to the circle.

Circle for all the emblems

BUTTERFLY

1. Use patterns to cut a circle from pale peach (or other color) felt, and a butterfly from a bright contrasting color.

2. To attach the butterfly, place it in the center of the circle and stitch through both layers of felt as you embroider the butterfly's body. Using brown embroidery floss, start at the top center and create three straight stitches half way down, plus another straight stitch from the middle to the bottom center of the butterfly. The head of the butterfly is a French knot and the antennae are stitched above the head.

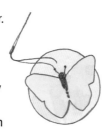

Heart

Butterfly

Each doll is designed with a symbol which might carry significance to the intended recipient: A heart to bring love, a butterfly to bring freedom and joy, a dandelion clock to grant a wish, a tree for strength, a moon and stars to bring light to darkness and sweet dreams, a rainbow to symbolize inner beauty and potential, a dove for peace. These are my own interpretations of the symbols, but you and the doll's recipient can make up your own story about the meaning.

Wings for the butterfly back

DANDELION CLOCK

1. Use patterns to cut a circle from pale yellow (or other color) felt and an oval from white felt.

Dandelion clock

2. Place the white oval near the top of the circle and, using light brown embroidery floss, create two small, straight stitches in the center of the white oval. While your needle is threaded with light brown, you can also create a small stitch below and slightly to one side of the white oval (this will be for a stray dandelion seed).

3. Thread your needle with off-white or ecru embroidery floss and create a series of straight stitches radiating from the center, about 4 mm (³/₁₆ in) per stitch. Cap every other stitch with three tiny stitches which radiate out from the end. While your needle is threaded with ecru embroidery floss, create a 4 mm (³/₁₆ in) stitch extending up from the stray stitch you embroidered below and cap with three tiny stitches.

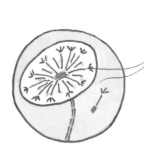

4. Finish your dandelion by threading your needle with green embroidery floss and delineate a stem by using backstitching.

TREE

1. Use the pattern to cut a circle from green felt.

2. Thread your needle with brown embroidery floss and create outlines using back stitch to delineate the shape of the trunk of your tree. Then fill in this outlined area with a series of short, straight stitches. The stitches which fill the interior of the tree trunk can be of differing lengths and slightly overlapping. This unevenness will give the effect of rough bark. Next, use back stitch to create branches radiating from the trunk.

3. Thread your needle with pale green embroidery floss and create tiny daisy stitches or small straight stitches to form leaves. Adding tiny French knots with red embroidery floss would turn this into an apple tree – a pretty variation to the design!

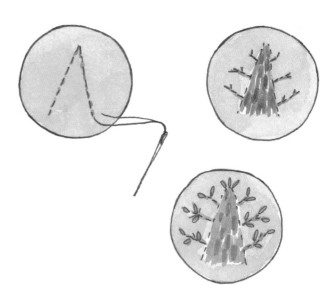

MOON

1. Use the patterns to cut a circle from blue felt and a moon from pale yellow.

Moon

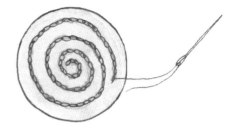

2. Use an appliqué stitch to attach the moon to the circle and stitch on a star-shaped sequin or embroider a star with a series of straight stitches.

3. Once the body of the doll is cut out, you can add a few more star-shaped sequins or embroidered stars.

DOVE OF PEACE

1. Use the patterns to cut a circle from lavender felt and the bird shape from white.

Dove

2. Use an appliqué stitch to attach the bird to the circle.

3. With brown embroidery floss make a tiny stitch to form the eye and a series of backstitches to form the olive branch. Thread your needle with pale green embroidery floss and create tiny daisy stitches or small straight stitches to form leaves. Note: *You can also make leaves using small straight stitches.*

RAINBOW

1. Use the pattern to cut a circle from lavender (or other color) felt.

2. I used embroidery floss with a rainbow variegation to create the chain stitched spiral for this doll. If you cannot find rainbow variegated embroidery floss, you can choose five or six tones and change colors at intervals to create a chain-stitched spiral. Alternatively, you could create a traditional arch-shaped rainbow using each of your rainbow colors.

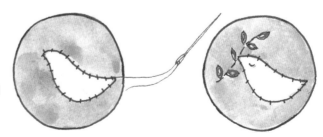

Sewing the body

1. Trim the pipe-cleaner wire to 20 cm (8 in) and bend according to diagram.

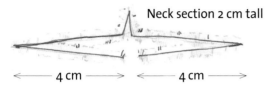

Neck section 2 cm tall

←— 4 cm —→ ←— 4 cm —→

2. Cut out two body pieces according to the pattern.

3. Appliqué the circular emblem to the stomach of one of the body pieces.

4. Place the two body pieces together and sew across the tops of the arms and shoulders, leaving space in the center to insert the pipe-cleaner wire neck.

5. Slip the neck portion of the pipe-cleaner wire through the neck-hole space at the top of the body, and then add the small wooden beads at the ends of the arms. If the arms seem too long or short, adjust the bends in the pipe-cleaner.

6. Starting on the right side, use a blanket stitch to sew beneath the arm and around the body. Stop sewing when you are 2 cm (¾ in) below the left arm and stuff the doll with herbs. Using a teaspoon will be helpful for adding small bits at a time. When the tip of the doll is filled with herbs, gently tamp the herbs down so that you have space to add more. Stuff until the doll is full and firm, then continue sewing the rest of the way up the body and under the arm.

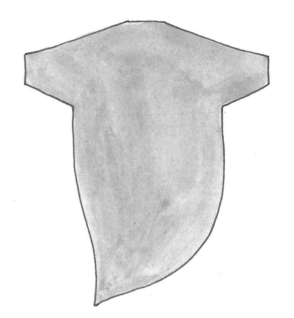

Body piece

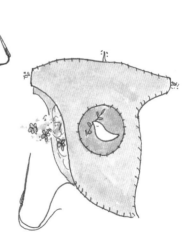

Adding the head and finishing the doll

1. Add the larger wooden bead to the neck, put the hat on the bead and draw or paint the face (the hat will help with placement of the facial features).

2. Remove the head, add a small amount of glue inside the hole and replace it on the pipe-cleaner neck. Note: *I recommend gluing the head after you are satisfied with the facial features. If you are not happy with them, you can always turn the bead around and try again. The hat will cover your first effort!*

3. Glue hat to the head.

4. Remove the two small beads from the ends of the arms, put a tiny amount of glue in the hole of each, and replace them again at the ends of the arms.

5. Cradle the finished doll gently against your cheek and seal it with love.

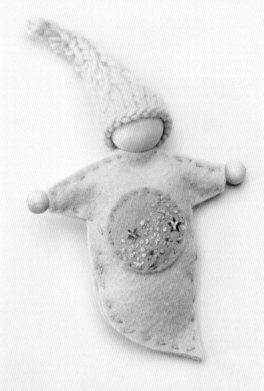

This past summer my mother was going through a difficult time and, knowing this, my older son wanted to make a doll for her. He pilfered an embroidery sample plus an extra doll hat from my work table and, with a little bit of guidance, was able to complete the rest of project himself. My mother was utterly delighted by this gift from her eldest grandson, and truly, his sweet gesture alone felt miraculously healing.

A Fairy-Garden Pincushion

While my seams and stitches are not nearly so fine as those made by fairies, I must confide in you that, since a little fairy has taken up residence on top of my pincushion, my sewing seems to go more smoothly. I can hardly feel cross when my embroidery floss tangles, and this little fairy is very clever at helping find lost pins.

SUPPLIES

3 cm (1³/₁₆ in) tot or baby/bee-shaped peg

Wool felt in two shades of green plus 3 additional colors for flowers

Tracing paper or a photocopy of patterns

Matching embroidery floss and needles

Glass seed-beads

PVA or other white craft glue

Watercolors (or paint of your choice) and brushes

Wool or other type of stuffing

1 large spoonful of sand

A funnel (or piece of paper which can be curved into a funnel-shape)

Pencils

Fabric scissors

Fairy Tears

A fairy sat deep in the heart of a rose,
And a tear trickled over the tip of her nose:
'Oh my! Oh my!' And she heaved a sigh.
'My wing it is broken, never more will I fly.'

But the rose whispered soft, 'Here's a needle so fine,
And our friend, Mr. Spider, a thread will entwine.
If you sew, sew, sew, make your fingers go,
You will mend it so neatly, it never will show.'

So that dear little fairy, the tears wiped away,
She stitched and she stitched through the long
summer day;
Then she laughed, 'Ha! Ha!' And she sang 'Tra la!
'Tis as good as when new, so I'm off, Ta ta!'

Margaret A. Sinclair

SMALL HELPING HANDS
- - - - - - - - - - - - - - - - - - -

This could be a fun project for a young person, newly introduced to sewing. Substituting a whip stitch or running stitch for the more complicated blanket stitch will make the sewing easier, and the flowers on top can be glued in place.

Making the pincushion

1. Cut out all pieces according to the patterns: three ovals,
one rectangle, approximately 15 blades of grass (optional),
seven or eight flowers in various shapes and colors.

Enlarge 200%
Actual size = 4 cm/1.5 in tall x 24 cm/9.5 in wide

Pincushion side
Cut 1

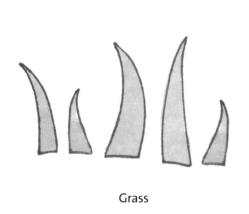

Grass

Flowers

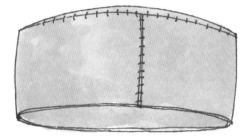

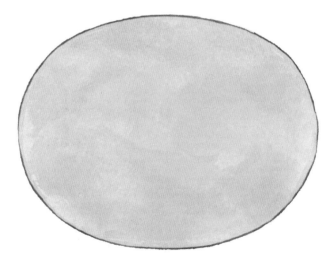

Pincushion top and bottom
Cut 3

2. Using a blanket stitch, sew the long edge of the rectangle around the curve of one of the oval shapes. This will be the top of your pincushion. Once you have stitched all the way around the oval, continue sewing a short way so that the edges of the rectangle overlap approximately ½ cm (¼ in). Trim any excess felt from the end of the rectangle and then use an appliqué stitch to seam down the overlapping edges.

3. Lay some of your felt flowers on the top of the cushion. It is tempting to add a lot of flowers; however, be mindful to leave space for some pins! Have fun trying out different arrangements for the flowers until it looks pleasing to you, and then use small embroidery stitches to tack everything down. I used daisy stitches to create tiny green leaves and decorate the flowers. Then I added a few beads here and there for extra sparkle. If you use a very small needle (approximately size 10) you can add the beads at the same time as you are adding embroidery without having to switch to a beading needle.

To add a flower which is not lying flat: fold a flower in half, and half again. Secure the folded flower with a stitch, and then secure to the top of the cushion with three or four additional stitches.

To add a bead, bring your needle through the felt to the right side of your work, insert the needle through the bead and then bring the needle back through the felt, near the spot where it emerged.

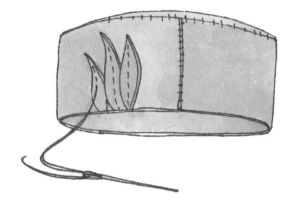

4. To attach blades of grass around the sides of your cushion, use a back stitch along the center of each blade. Note: *The points should be facing up towards the oval you have already sewn.*

5. Using a blanket stitch, sew the remaining two ovals of green felt to the pincushion. Leave 5 cm (2 in) open so you can add stuffing.

6. Insert the end of a funnel (or piece of paper curved into a funnel shape) between the bottom two layers of the pin cushion and add a spoonful of very dry sand. This will keep the pincushion stable. Pin shut the opening where you added the sand and then stuff the main section of the pincushion. It is best to stuff it firmly; however, if the cushion has been sewn by a child, you may want to stuff it more lightly so as not to strain any seams made with wider stitches. Once the cushion has been stuffed, sew up the remaining 5 cm (2 in).

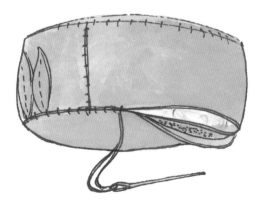

Decorating the doll

1. Prior to painting, you may choose to give your doll a quick once-over with some sandpaper to smooth any rough portions (especially on the head of the doll where you plan to draw or paint a face).

2. Paint the hair and body of your doll. Add a face with paint or pencil. If you used watercolor paint, you can apply a small amount of beeswax polish to the hair and body. Note: *I don't recommend using polish on the face as it can cause the paint to smudge.*

3. Have fun trying out different embellishments on your doll. I glued a tiny flower to the back of my doll's head, but you might choose to add a flower to the top of her head to form a little hat.

4. If you are using a peg doll with a narrow base (i.e. a baby/bee-shaped doll), put a small amount of glue on a felt flower and curve it around the base of the doll. This will add stability to a doll with a narrow base. Next, for all shape dolls, glue the base of your fairy to a larger-size felt flower. Once the glue is dry, you can attach the doll to the top of the cushion by putting pins through the petals of the flower.

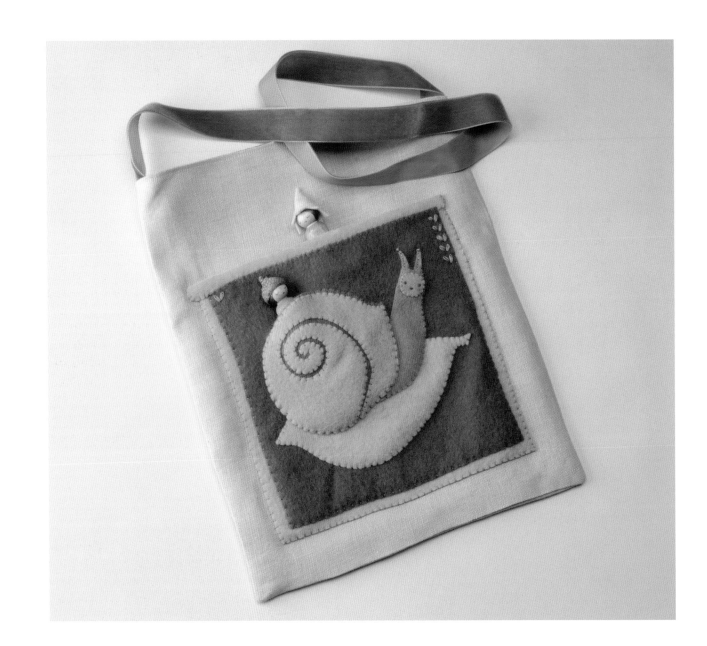

A Snail-Rider Gathering Bag

There are many ways a fairy could travel – on the back of a bird, butterfly, dragonfly or frog, by grasping the stem of wind-blown leaf or dandelion seed, but if I were a fairy, I think I would travel by snail. Traveling by snail-back might not be the most efficient mode of transportation, but the slow pace would lend itself to enjoying the scenery. Gliding slowly past, a fairy could admire sparkling blades of grass, acorn caps, twigs and fallen pine cones, pretty pebbles, moss and tree roots. It seems to me, this is much the same pace one travels when walking with a small child – and when the child stops to examine every small thing in his path, so the adult must slow her pace too!

Thinking about snails, small children and slow-paced walks, I sized this bag to be carried by a child. It can be used for collecting treasures along the way, for carrying a book or bringing along a snack. There is a little pocket in the shell of the snail to hold a peg-doll friend; however, during longer journeys (or in case of cartwheels, somersaults and twirling), the peg doll might prefer to ride in the larger pocket so she doesn't fall out and get lost.

SUPPLIES

4 cm (1⅝ in) boy-peg

½ meter (½ yard) natural color linen or other fabric of your choice

½ meter (½ yard) quilting-weight cotton fabric for lining

Wool felt: two tones of green, two tones of light brown and two colorful tones for the shell

1 m (1 yd) velvet or grosgrain ribbon, 2.2 cm (1 in) wide

Tracing paper or a photocopy of patterns

Sewing needles, matching thread, embroidery floss

A sewing machine (optional)

Watercolors (or paint of your choice) and brushes

Rotary cutter and mat (optional)

Fabric scissors

Sandpaper

Beeswax polish

PVA or other white craft glue

SMALL HELPING HANDS

- - - - - - - - - - - - - - - - - -

A small child will enjoy painting her own companion to ride the snail on the pocket of this bag, while a slightly older child might be able to help appliqué the snail (for this, a child could use a running stitch, or whichever stitch she finds easiest). Choosing the colors for the snail shell is fun too.

Constructing the pocket

1. Cut out all the pieces for the pocket from felt: pattern pieces A and B, top reinforcement strip, one leaf, one snail body, one snail face, and two shell pieces and two small pocket pieces.

Top reinforcement strip

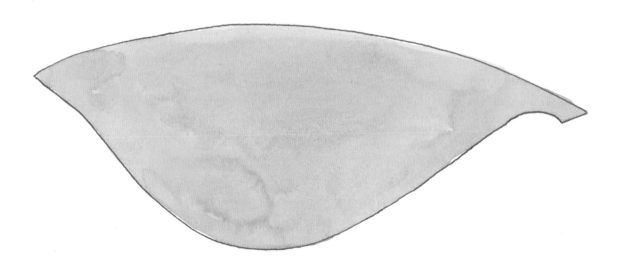

Leaf

Pocket piece A (16.5 cm/6.5 in square)
Cut 1

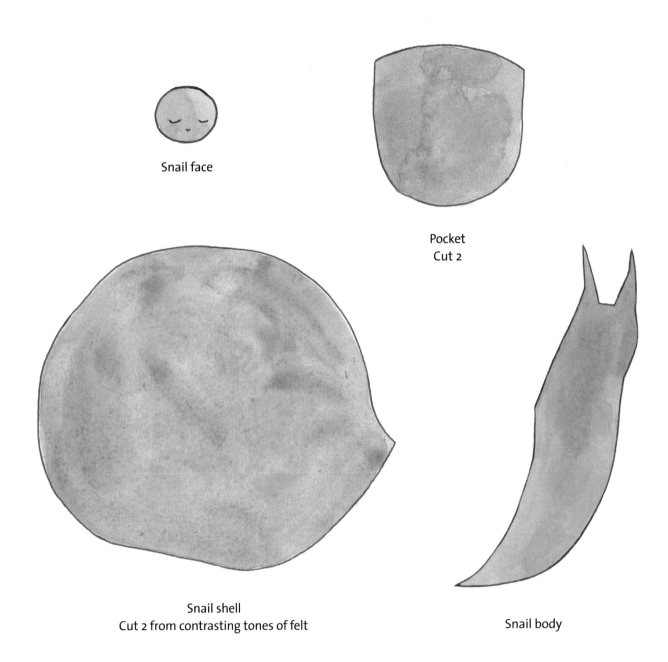

Snail face

Pocket
Cut 2

Snail shell
Cut 2 from contrasting tones of felt

Snail body

Pocket piece B (18 cm/7 in square)
Cut 1

2. Arrange the leaf and other pieces for your snail on piece A. Adjust until you are satisfied with the placement. Then pin the leaf in place and sew around the perimeter using an appliqué stitch.

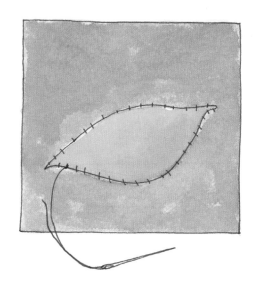

3. Pin a paper pattern piece for the shell with a tracing of the spiral to one of your felt snail shells. Cut through the paper and felt along the spiral. Unpin the paper and cut along the spiral again, removing approximately 3 mm (1/8 in) from the inside edge of the spiral. Pin the spiral-cut shell piece to the uncut piece and, using an appliqué stitch, sew down the edges of the spiral.

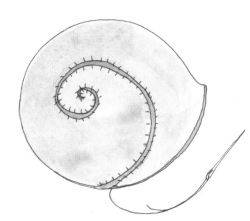

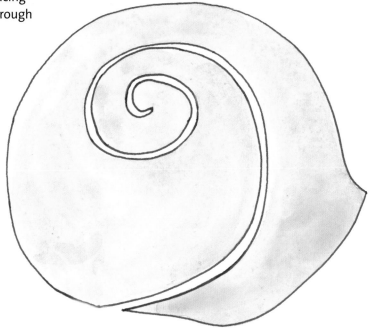

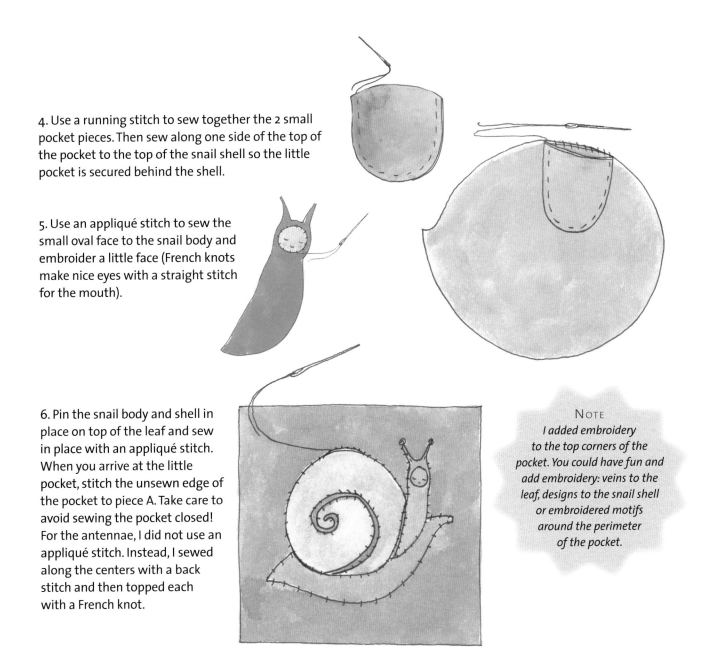

4. Use a running stitch to sew together the 2 small pocket pieces. Then sew along one side of the top of the pocket to the top of the snail shell so the little pocket is secured behind the shell.

5. Use an appliqué stitch to sew the small oval face to the snail body and embroider a little face (French knots make nice eyes with a straight stitch for the mouth).

6. Pin the snail body and shell in place on top of the leaf and sew in place with an appliqué stitch. When you arrive at the little pocket, stitch the unsewn edge of the pocket to piece A. Take care to avoid sewing the pocket closed! For the antennae, I did not use an appliqué stitch. Instead, I sewed along the centers with a back stitch and then topped each with a French knot.

NOTE
I added embroidery to the top corners of the pocket. You could have fun and add embroidery: veins to the leaf, designs to the snail shell or embroidered motifs around the perimeter of the pocket.

7. Sew the square edge of the reinforcement strip to one edge of pocket piece B (see diagram) then fold the strip over the top of piece B and stitch down on the front side.

Note: *The reinforcement strip is optional, but it will make the pocket more durable.*

8. Center piece A onto the front (or right) side of piece B, with the top of piece A overlapping the rounded edge of the reinforcement strip. Sew around the edges of piece A using an appliqué stitch.

Note: *Piece A will be sewn across the top to the reinforcement strip.*

Making the bag

1. Cut two pieces of linen (or other fabric) for the main body of the bag 25.5 cm (10 in) by 30.5 cm (12 in) and two rectangles of the same measurements from quilting-weight cotton for the lining.

Snail bag linen
Enlarge 200%
Actual size = 25.5 cm/10 in wide x 30.5 cm/12 in tall
Cut 2

Snail bag lining
Enlarge 200%
Actual size = 25.5 cm/10 in wide x 30.5 cm/12 in tall
Cut 2

2. Pin the appliquéd pocket to one piece of linen and sew down by machine or with an appliqué stitch on three sides.

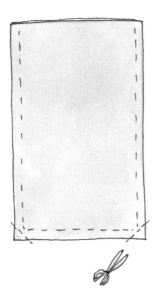

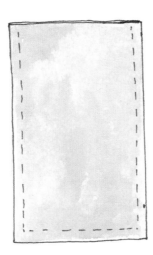

3. Pin the two pieces of linen together with the pocket on the inside and, using a sewing machine, stitch around three sides with a 1 cm (½ in) seam allowance. Pin the right sides of the quilting cotton together and sew around three sides with a 1 cm (½ in) seam allowance. Clip the extra fabric from the corners of the linen, turn right side out and use an iron to flatten along the seams.

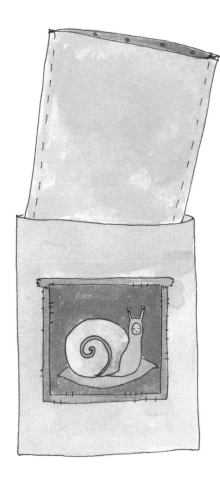

4. Slip the lining inside the linen bag. Match up the seams, then fold in 1 cm (½ in) along the top edges of the linen and lining and pin together.

5. Trim the velvet or grosgrain ribbon for the strap to desired length and slip the ends into either side of the bag, next to the seams, between the linen and the lining. Pin the ribbon in place and then sew the linen and lining together around the top opening of the bag.

6. If you wish, you can add snap fasteners to the top of the large pocket or the top of the bag.

Decorating the doll

1. Prior to painting, you may choose to give your doll a quick once-over with some sandpaper to smooth any rough portions (especially on the head of the doll where you plan to draw or paint a face).

2. Paint the hair and body of your doll. Add a face with paint or pencil. If you used watercolor paint, you can apply a small amount of beeswax polish to the hair and body. Note: *I don't recommend using polish on the face as it can cause the paint to smudge.*

3. Glue on an acorn cap for a hat, or make a flower-gnome cap. To make the gnome cap, cut out wool felt according to the pattern. Overlap the two straight sides, adjust to fit the head of the doll and, using a flat appliqué stitch, sew to form a cone shape. Attach the cap to the head of your doll with a small amount of glue.

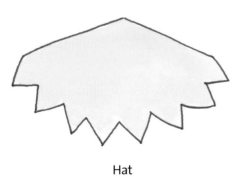

Hat

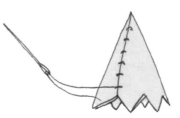

Greenwood Tree Wall Hanging

Come, follow, follow, follow, follow, follow, follow me.
Whither shall I follow, follow, follow, whither shall I follow, follow thee?
To the greenwood, to the greenwood, to the greenwood, greenwood tree. Traditional round (John Hilton the younger)

SUPPLIES

6 cm (2³⁄₈ in) standard wood-people peg

5 cm (2 in) angel-peg

4 cm (1⁵⁄₈ in) boy-pegs

½ meter (½ yard) light green felt

½ meter (½ yard) brown felt

½ meter (½ yard) square darker green felt

½ meter (½ yard) square sky blue felt

Smaller amounts of wool felt: white, red, bright green and pale yellow, light brown, and gray, etc.

Sewing needles and matching embroidery floss in a variety of colors

Wool roving in white and gray, a felting needle and foam felting pad

Yarn or ribbon for hanging the project on the wall

Tracing paper or a photocopy of patterns

Watercolors (or paint of your choice) and brushes

Rotary cutter and mat (optional)

Wood dowel and two dowel caps (ball-style or finial-style)

Fabric scissors

Sandpaper

Beeswax polish

Inside the trunk of this magical greenwood tree there lives a sleepy owl, and at the roots, you will meet two rabbits scampering with their friend Toadstool-the-Gnome. If you look closely, you can also find a shy dandelion fairy. She is very clever at hiding, but whisper to her softly, and she might peek out from beneath her gossamer bonnet to say hello.

I've made this tree with a few bright springtime leaves, but the tree and hillsides can easily be customized to reflect your favorite season. Perhaps the tree on your wall hanging will bear pink springtime blossoms, red apples, or golden autumn leaves. Maybe your hillsides will be covered with daisies, or buttercups...

SMALL HELPING HANDS

- - - - - - - - - - - - - - - - - - - -

An older child could help with the long seams attaching the plain felt backing (substitute a running stitch if mastering the appliqué stitch is too difficult), and needle-felting the clouds would be a fun job for any child old enough to safely use needles.

A younger child might enjoy painting the dowel (plus end-caps) which will be used for hanging the project, and of course, even the smallest hands will enjoy creating some peg dolls!

Making the wall hanging

1. Cut all pieces according to the patterns: large and small backings, sky, front meadow, left hillside, tree, tree-hole pocket, leaves, grass, dandelions, toadstool pieces and six small pocket pieces.

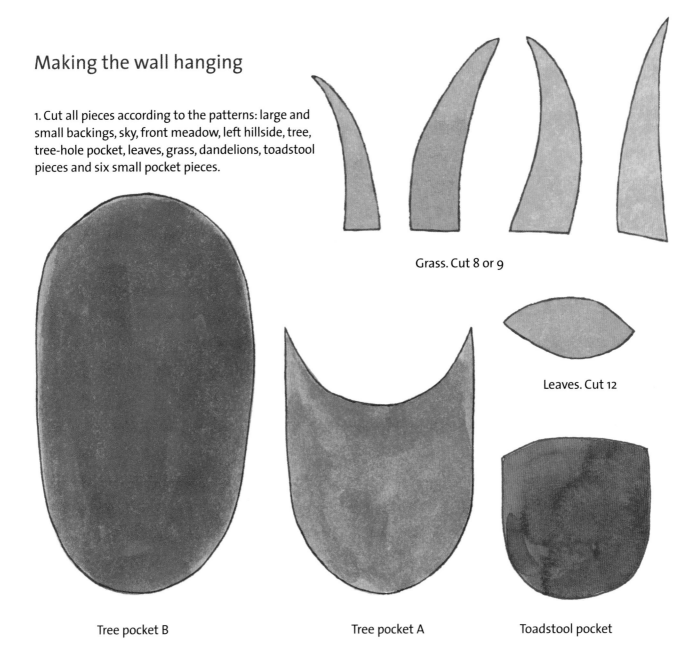

Grass. Cut 8 or 9

Leaves. Cut 12

Tree pocket B

Tree pocket A

Toadstool pocket

Green backing
Enlarge 200%
Actual size = 37 cm/14.5 in tall x 32 cm/12.5 in wide

Brown backing
Enlarge 200%
Actual size = 30.5 cm/12 in square

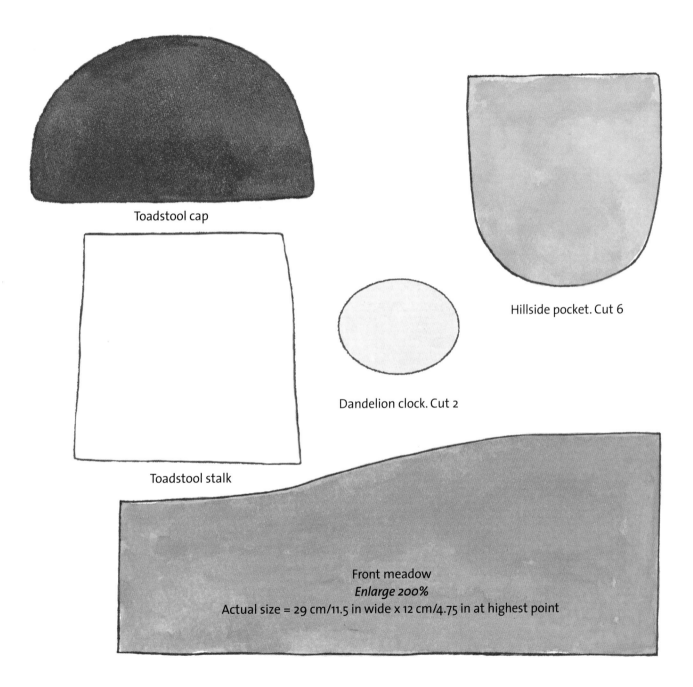

Toadstool cap

Toadstool stalk

Dandelion clock. Cut 2

Hillside pocket. Cut 6

Front meadow
Enlarge 200%
Actual size = 29 cm/11.5 in wide x 12 cm/4.75 in at highest point

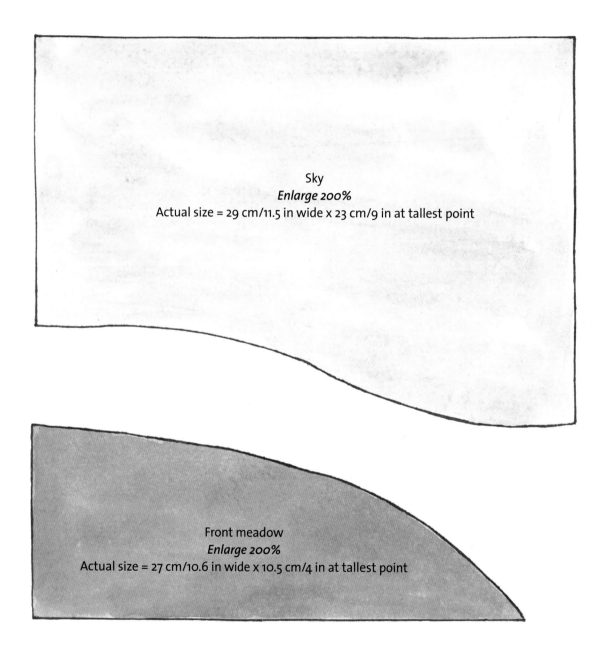

Sky
Enlarge 200%
Actual size = 29 cm/11.5 in wide x 23 cm/9 in at tallest point

Front meadow
Enlarge 200%
Actual size = 27 cm/10.6 in wide x 10.5 cm/4 in at tallest point

Tree
Enlarge 200%
Actual size = 29.5 cm/11.6 in tall
Tree trunk 23cm/9 in wide at base

2. Spread apart the fibers of three wisps of white wool roving. Place the piece of sky blue felt on a thick foam felting block and arrange the roving in cloud-like formations. Use a multi-needle tool to mesh the fibers of the roving to the sky blue backing.

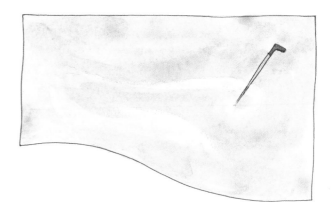

3. Place the sky section over the smaller backing piece (brown) so that the backing is visible, approximately ½ cm (¼ in) around the edges. Sew in place with an appliqué stitch.

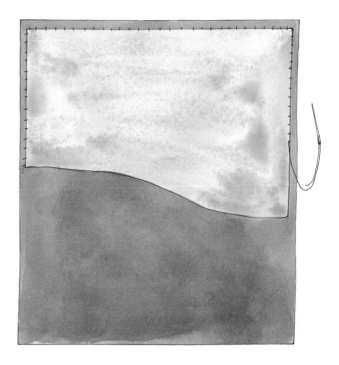

Note
I completed all the sewing for this project by hand, but, if you prefer, the long seams could easily be done on a sewing machine.

4. Sew together the six green pocket pieces to form three small pockets. Sew one pocket along a top edge to the wrong side of the left hillside as indicated in the diagram. Sew each of the other two pockets along a top edge to the wrong side of the front meadow (as indicated in the front meadow diagram). Be sure to stitch across the top of only one side of each pocket so the pockets are not sewn shut! Note: *The pockets should be stitched 1–2 cm (½–1 in) from the side edges of the front meadow and back hillside. If the pockets are placed close to the center, there will not be adequate space for the tree trunk in the middle of the wall hanging.*

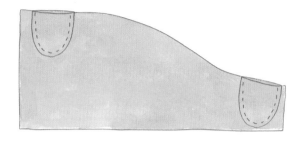

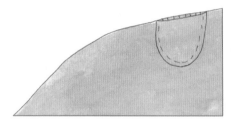

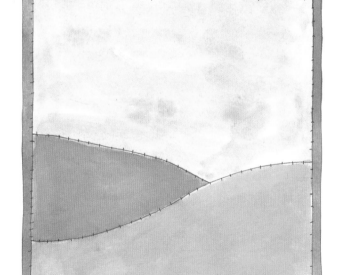

5. Arrange the front meadow and back hillside so that the brown backing is visible, approximately ½ cm (¼ in) around the edges. Sew in place with an appliqué stitch. When you arrive at a pocket, sew along the back edge of the pocket to attach it to the piece behind it.

6. Sew tree-pocket piece A to piece B as indicated in the diagram. Then sew the top edge of piece A to the bottom edge of the hole in the tree, and the top of B around the top of the hole. (This might not make sense as you read through these instructions; however, if you put a doll into the pocket formed by pattern pieces A & B, and then place the pocket behind the tree with the doll peeking through the hole in the tree, the instructions might seem clearer!)

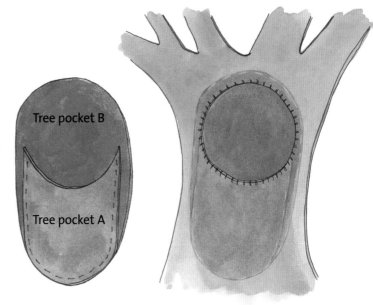

Tree pocket B

Tree pocket A

7. To create the toadstool, start by needle-felting, embroidering or appliquéing white spots onto the toadstool cap pattern piece. Place the cap over the stem, overlapping ½ cm (¼ in) and then stitch the cap to the stem using an appliqué stitch. If you would like any blades of grass to overlap the toadstool, sew them onto the toadstool now. Finally, sew the two toadstool pocket pieces together and then stitch one edge of the pocket across the top to the wrong side of the toadstool cap. Be sure to stitch across the top of only one side of the pocket so it is not sewn shut!

8. To create dandelions, thread your needle with light brown or yellow embroidery floss and make three, four or five small, straight stitches in the center of each white or pale yellow oval. Then, using white or ecru embroidery floss, create a series of straight stitches radiating from the center, approximately 5 mm (½ in) per stitch. Or, instead of making dandelions, you could cut out different flower shapes in bright colors and embroider them in various ways.

9. After you have sewn the pocket behind the tree, constructed the toadstool pocket and embroidered your flowers, arrange the tree trunk, toadstool, flowers and grass blades on the wall hanging. When you are satisfied with the arrangement, pin everything in place.

10. Start by sewing down the smaller items: Using an appliqué stitch, sew down the sides of the toadstool cap and stem. Using a back stitch, sew down the centers of the grass blades and use a blanket or appliqué stitch to sew around the flowers. Note: *If you are appliquéing on an area of the front meadow where a pocket is sewn behind it, be careful to avoid sewing the pocket closed!*

11. Once the small pieces are sewn down, use an appliqué stitch to sew down the trunk and branches of the tree. When this is done, back stitch down the centers of the leaves, securing them at various intervals along the branches.

12. Place your wall hanging over the larger rectangular backing piece so that 0.5 cm (¼ in) is visible around the bottom and side edges. Pin in place and then sew down using an appliqué stitch.

13. To create a casing to hold the dowel for hanging, fold the top edge back so that 0.5 cm (¼ in) of the larger backing is visible at the top. Pin and sew in place across the back.

14. Cut a dowel 33.5 cm (13 ½ in), insert into casing at the top of the wall hanging and glue a dowel cap at each end.

Decorating the owl

1. I have created my owl using a 6 cm (2 ³⁄₈ in) standard wood-people peg. Prior to painting, you may choose to give your doll a quick once-over with some sandpaper to smooth any rough portions (especially on the head where you plan to draw or paint a face).

2. Paint the body and head gray, leaving an unpainted oval for the face. Then, add a face inside the oval and paint some darker gray feathers on the chest and stomach.

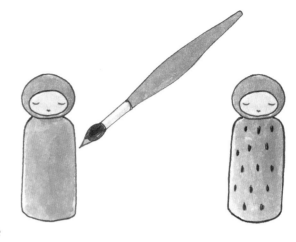

Hat back

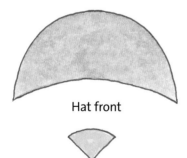

Hat front

Beak

Wing. Cut 2

3. To create the hat, cut out front and back pieces from gray wool felt. Align the pieces along the curve of the top of the hat and then, using embroidery floss, sew around the top. To create the ear tufts, take a tiny wisp of gray wool roving and fold the fibers of the roving in half and half again. Then place the hat on a thick piece of dense foam and place your little fiber bundle on one of the pointed ears. With your felting needle, start stabbing one end of your little fiber bundle through the felt of one of the little points on top of the hat. Between stabs, use your needle to pull straying wisps of fiber in towards the felt point where you are securing your fibers. When you are satisfied that your fibers are secured, use sharp scissors to trim the fibers at the sides and across the top of the wispy little ear tuft. Repeat the process for the other ear tuft.

Note: *If you don't have needle-felting materials on hand, you could either stitch fuzzy bits of yarn in place, add a small bit of feather, or leave the ear-tufts plain (the peaks at the sides of the hat are very cute, even unadorned).*

4. With two strands of gray embroidery floss, sew a running stitch along the bottom edge of the back of the hat and gather slightly to fit the contours of the doll's head. Glue the hat onto the doll and add the yellow beak piece to the front of the hat at the center.

5. Cut out the wings and glue them to the sides of the doll.

Decorating the rabbit

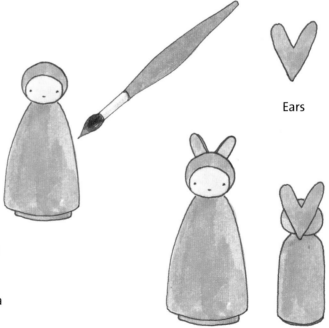

Ears

1. Prior to painting, you may choose to give your doll a quick once-over with some sandpaper to smooth any rough portions (especially on the head of the doll where you plan to draw or paint a face).

2. Paint the head and body of your doll brown, leaving an oval space for the face. Add facial features with paint or pencil. If you used watercolor paint, you can apply a small amount of beeswax polish to the painted areas if you wish. Note: *I don't recommend using polish on the face as it can cause the paint to smudge.*

3. Cut out rabbit ears according to the pattern and use a small bit of glue to secure to the back of the head.

Decorating the toadstool gnome

1. This toadstool gnome is created from a 4 cm (1 ⅝ in) boy-peg. Prior to painting, you may choose to give your doll a quick once-over with some sandpaper to smooth any rough portions (especially on the head of the doll where you plan to draw or paint a face).

2. Using opaque acrylic paint for the cap (or thick watercolor paint diluted with very little water), paint a red cap over the head. Once the red paint is dry, use an opaque white acrylic paint to add dots to the cap.

3. Add facial features with paint or pencil.

4. For the body, blend white paint downwards, fading into a light brown.

Decorating the dandelion flower fairy

1. This flower fairy is created from a 4 cm (1 ⅝ in) boy-peg. Prior to painting, you may choose to give your doll a quick once-over with some sandpaper to smooth any rough portions (especially on the head of the doll where you plan to draw or paint a face).

2. Paint the hair and body of your doll. Add a face with paint or pencil. If you used watercolor paint, you can apply a small amount of beeswax polish to the hair and bodies if you wish. Note: *I don't recommend using polish on the face as it can cause the paint to smudge.*

3. To create a dandelion 'bonnet' cut two white ovals according to the pattern and embroider each one separately as follows: Thread your needle with light brown or yellow embroidery floss and make three, four or five small, straight stitches in the center of each oval. Then, using ecru embroidery floss, create a series of straight stitches radiating from the center, approximately 5 mm (½ in) per stitch. Once each oval is embroidered, place them back to back and, using a blanket stitch, sew around the perimeter. Use glue to attach to the back of the fairy's head.

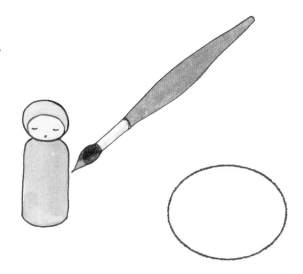

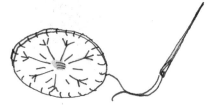

Bonnet. Cut 2

Pirates & Merfolk Wall Hanging

SUPPLIES

5 cm (2 in) angel-pegs

4 cm (1⅝ in) boy-pegs

½ meter (½ yard) dark blue felt

½ meter (½ yard) square medium blue felt

½ meter (½ yard) square sky blue felt

½ meter (½ yard) square additional shade of green or blue felt (for backing)

Smaller amounts of wool felt: white, red, gray, black, brown and various shades of blue and green

Sewing needles and matching embroidery floss in a variety of colors

Wool roving in white, a felting needle and foam felting pad

Yarn or ribbon for hanging the project on the wall

Tracing paper or a photocopy of patterns

Watercolors (or paint of your choice) and brushes

Rotary cutter and mat (optional)

Wood dowel and two dowel caps (ball-style or finial-style)

Fabric scissors

Sandpaper

Beeswax polish

PVA or other white craft glue

Pirate Story

Where shall we adventure, to-day that we're afloat,
Wary of the weather and steering by a star?
Shall it be to Africa, a-steering of the boat,
To Providence, or Babylon, or off to Malabar?

Robert Louis Stevenson

SMALL HELPING HANDS

- - - - - - - - - - - - - - - - - -

Small hands will have a wonderful time creating pirates to sail this ship and mermaids to dive among the waves. Young children will also enjoy painting the dowel and end-caps used for hanging the project.

An older child could help with the long seams attaching the plain felt backing (substitute a running stitch if mastering the appliqué stitch is too difficult) or maybe even try his or her hand at stitching a dolphin.

Making the wall hanging

1. Cut all pieces according to the patterns: large and small backings, sky, front waves, back waves, rock, ship, sails, portholes, masts, flag, plus all pocket pieces.

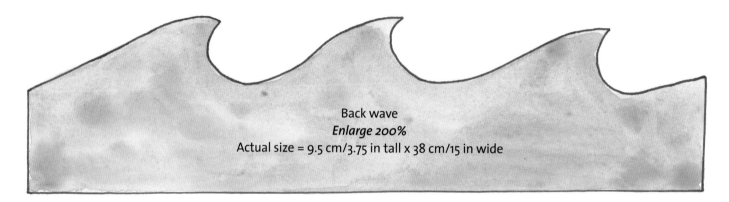

Back wave
Enlarge 200%
Actual size = 9.5 cm/3.75 in tall x 38 cm/15 in wide

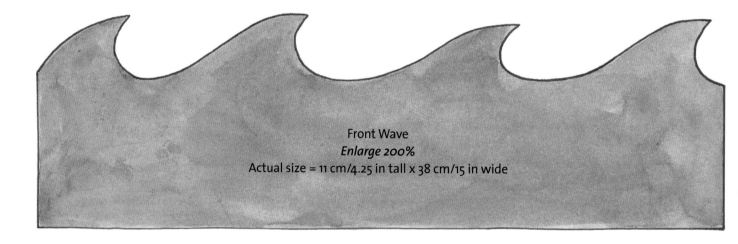

Front Wave
Enlarge 200%
Actual size = 11 cm/4.25 in tall x 38 cm/15 in wide

Larger blue backing
Enlarge 400%
Actual size = 40.5 cm/16 in wide x 38 cm/15 in tall

Sky
Enlarge 400%
Actual size = 37.5 cm/14.75 in wide x 24 cm/9.5 in tall

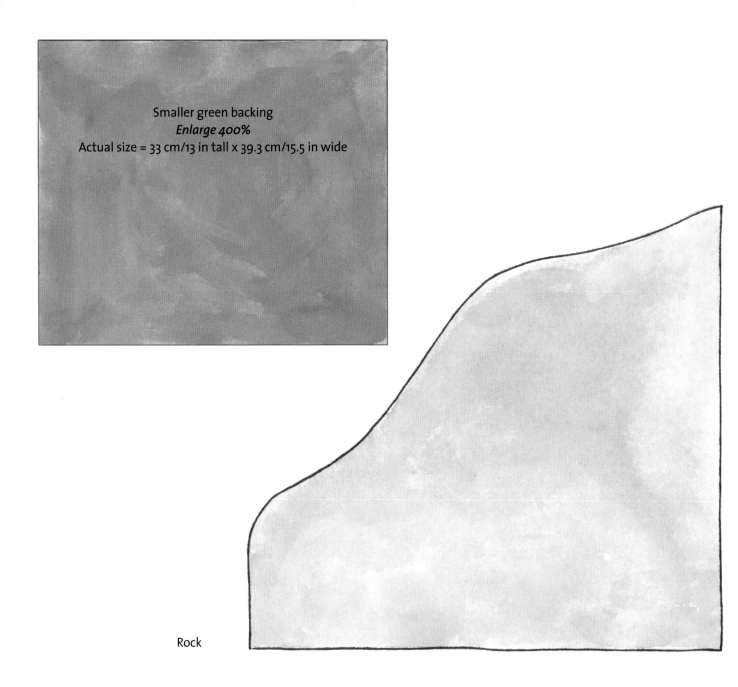

Smaller green backing
Enlarge 400%
Actual size = 33 cm/13 in tall x 39.3 cm/15.5 in wide

Rock

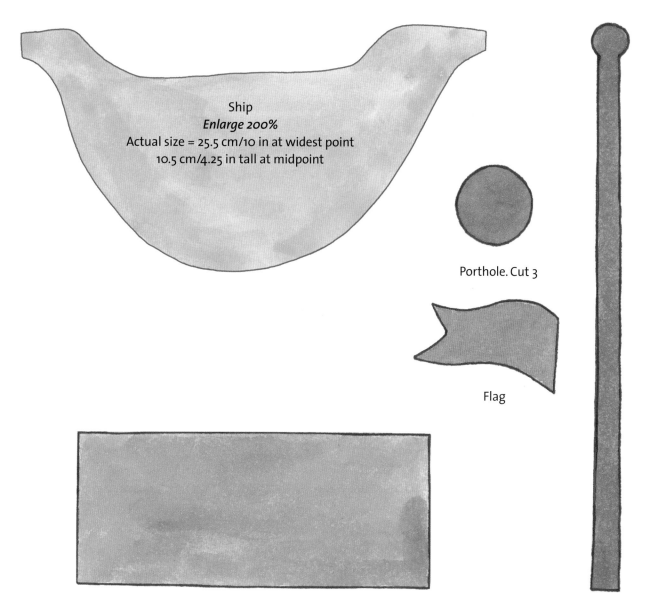

Ship
Enlarge 200%
Actual size = 25.5 cm/10 in at widest point
10.5 cm/4.25 in tall at midpoint

Porthole. Cut 3

Flag

Ship pocket. Cut 2

Mast. Cut 2

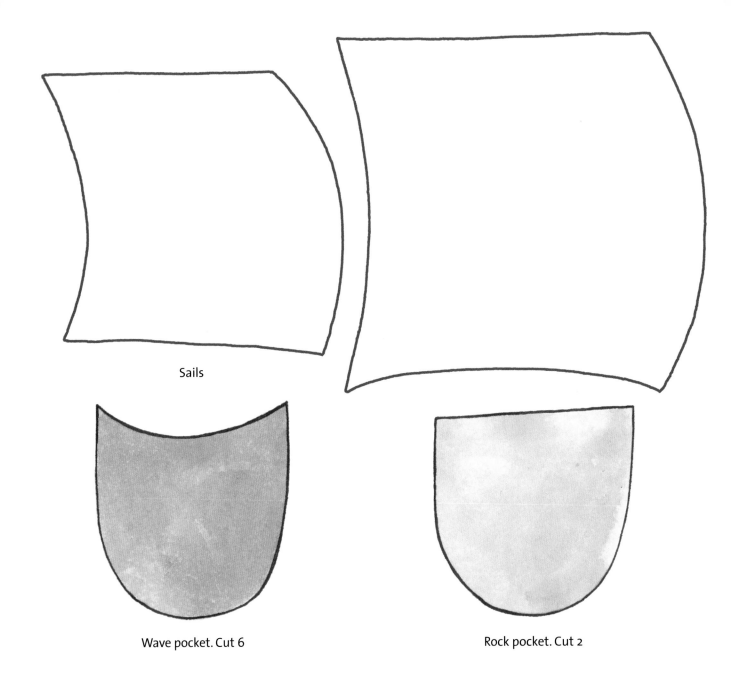

Sails

Wave pocket. Cut 6

Rock pocket. Cut 2

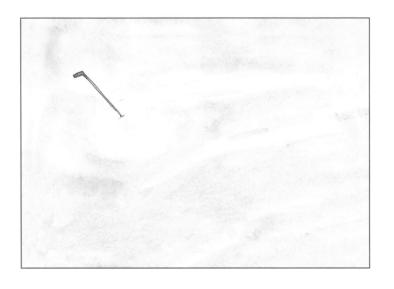

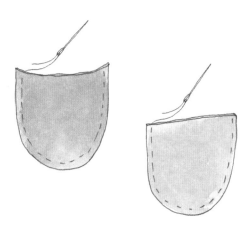

2. Spread apart the fibers of three wisps of white wool roving. Place the piece of sky blue felt over a thick foam felting block and arrange the roving in cloud-like formations. Use a multi-needle tool to mesh the fibers of the roving to the sky blue backing.

4. Create pockets for the ship, rock and waves by pairing up the pieces and sewing together with a running stitch.

3. Appliqué portholes onto the ship.

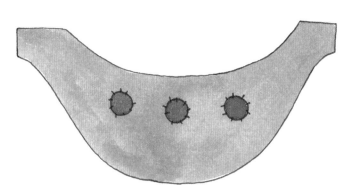

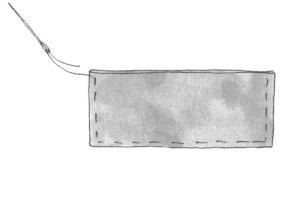

5. Sew the gray pocket along one top edge to the wrong side of the rock as indicated in the diagram. Sew the wide brown pocket along one top edge to the wrong side of the ship as indicated in the diagram, and sew the three blue pockets to the wrong side of front wave piece (as similarly indicated in the diagram). Be sure to stitch across the top of only one side of each pocket so the pockets are not sewn shut!

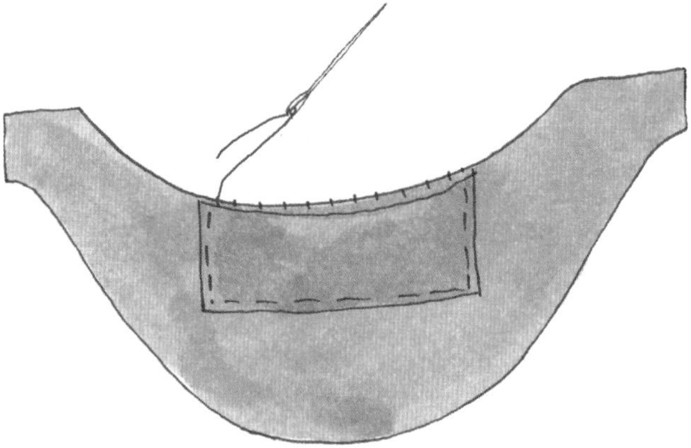

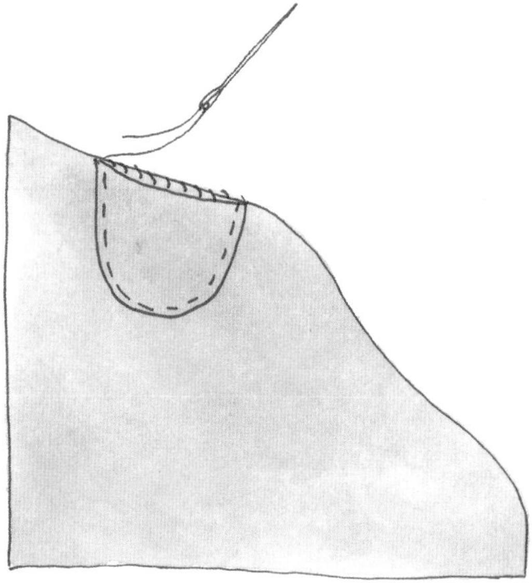

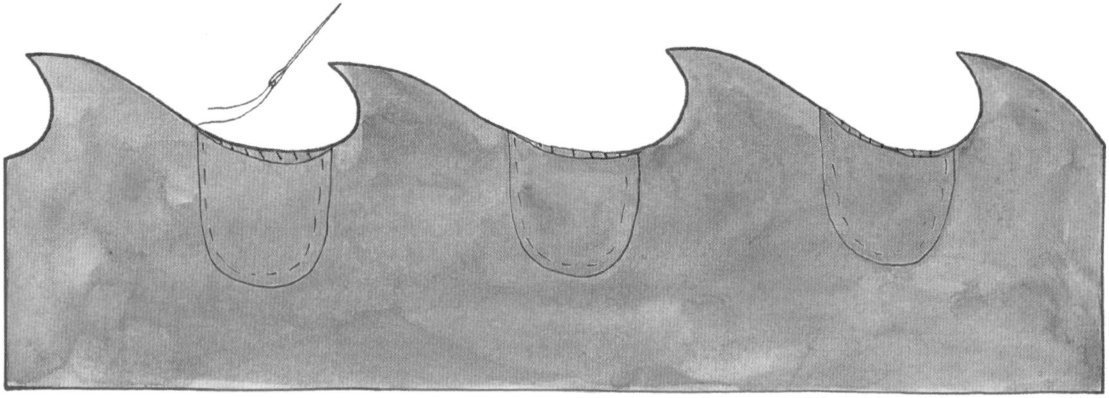

6. Place the sky section over the smaller backing piece (gray-green) so that the backing is visible approximately ½ cm (¼ in) around the edges. Sew in place with an appliqué stitch.

7. Arrange all other pieces (rock, ship, masts, sails and waves) on the wall hanging so that the backing shows 0.5 cm (¼ in) around the sides and bottom edges of the waves (and so the bottom edge of the rock is covered by the waves). When you are satisfied with the arrangement, secure the ship, masts, sails, flag and rock with pins, set the waves aside and then, using an appliqué stitch, sew down the pieces you have pinned. Note: *I added a little bit of stuffing inside the sails to give them the appearance of being billowed by the wind.*

8. Arrange the waves over the rock and bottom of the ship again, so that the backing shows 0.5 cm (¼ in) around the sides and bottom edges (and so the bottom edge of the rock is covered by the waves). Using an appliqué stitch, sew down the waves. When you arrive at a section of the waves where there is a pocket, sew down the back of the pocket to the material behind it, and then continue appliquéing the main portion of the waves.

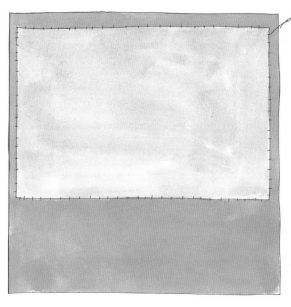

9. Place your wall hanging over the larger rectangular backing piece so that 0.5 cm (¼ in) is visible around the bottom and side edges. Pin in place and then sew down using an appliqué stitch.

10. To create a casing to hold the dowel for hanging, fold the top edge back so that 0.5 cm (¼ in) of the larger backing is visible at the top. Pin and sew in place across the back.

11. Cut a dowel 33.5 cm (13 ½ in), insert into casing at the top of the wall hanging and glue a dowel cap at each end.

Decorating a pirate

1. Prior to painting, you may choose to give your doll a quick once-over with some sandpaper to smooth any rough portions (especially on the head of the doll where you plan to draw or paint a face).

2. Paint the clothing of your pirate. I like the look of brown or gray trousers, a striped shirt of red and white, and a black belt, but you may have other ideas about how to dress your pirate. After the clothing is painted, add hair and facial features.

3. To add a coat, cut out from black felt according to the pattern. If you wish, you can decorate the front of the coat by embroidering or sewing beads to look like rows of buttons. Add a little bit of glue on the inside of the coat, wrap around the back of the doll and secure with a stitch or two at the front.

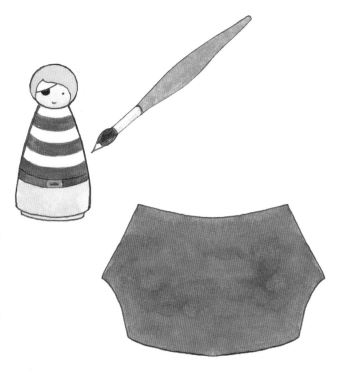

Coat

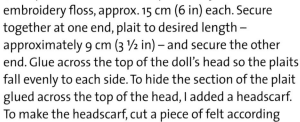

Headscarf

4. For plaits, start with three pieces of yarn or embroidery floss, approx. 15 cm (6 in) each. Secure together at one end, plait to desired length – approximately 9 cm (3 ½ in) – and secure the other end. Glue across the top of the doll's head so the plaits fall evenly to each side. To hide the section of the plait glued across the top of the head, I added a headscarf. To make the headscarf, cut a piece of felt according to the pattern, secure around the head with a tiny bit of glue and then stitch or bind the two ends of the headscarf together with embroidery floss.

Making a merchild

1. Prior to painting, you may choose to give your doll a quick once-over with some sandpaper to smooth any rough portions (especially on the head of the doll where you plan to draw or paint a face).

2. Paint the hair and body of your doll. Add a face with paint or pencil. If you used watercolor paint, you can apply a small amount of beeswax polish to the hair and body if you wish. Note: *I don't recommend using polish on the face as it can cause the paint to smudge.*

3. Cut a tail according to the pattern and glue to the back of your doll.

4. If you would like to add plaits, refer to instructions within the section for making a pirate.

5. To make the mermaid hat, cut out wool felt according to the pattern. Overlap the two straight sides, adjust to fit the head of the doll and, using a flat appliqué fell stitch, sew to form a cone shape. Tack the point of the cone down at the back to form a bonnet. Put a small amount of glue inside the hat and place on the head of the doll. For a bit of panache, you can decorate the hat with a tiny seashell.

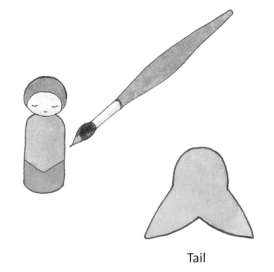

Tail

Hat

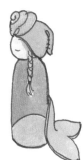

Making an octopus

1. I used a 4 cm (1 ⅝ in) boy-peg for this doll. Prior to painting, you may choose to give your doll a quick once-over with some sandpaper to smooth any rough portions (especially on the head of the doll where you plan to draw or paint a face).

2. Paint the head and upper half of the body red, leaving an oval space for the face. Paint the lower half of the body black and add facial features inside the unpainted oval. If you used watercolor paint on the body, you can apply a small amount of beeswax polish to the painted areas if you wish. Note: *I don't recommend using polish on the face as it can cause the paint to smudge.*

3. Cut out the tentacles according to the pattern and use a line of glue to secure the tentacles around the body.

Tentacles

Making a dolphin

1. Cut the shapes from felt according to the patterns: a white underside and gray body and tail.

2. Fold the body in half (down the front of the beak at the center) to match up the fins. Using a blanket stitch, sew along the back (and dorsal fin).

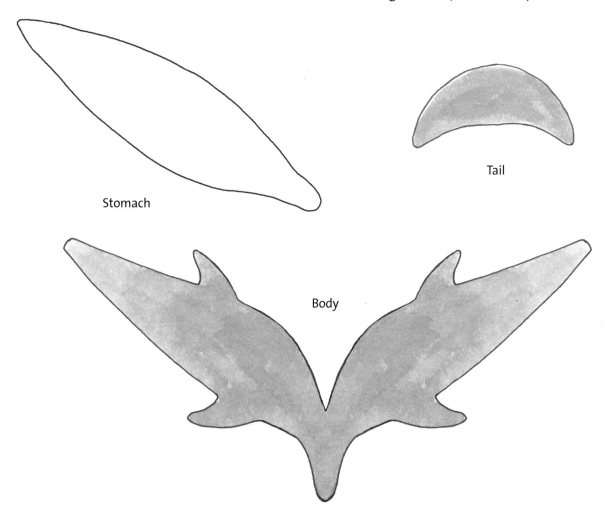

Stomach

Tail

Body

3. Align the beaks of the gray piece and white stomach piece. Carefully pin together at the sides, allowing the pectoral fins to stick out. Insert the tail flukes between the white and gray sections and pin in place. Then, using a blanket stitch, sew up the sides of the dolphin, leaving a 3 cm (1 ¼ in) opening. Add stuffing and close the seam.

4. To decide on the position for the eyes, place pins in the sides of the head. When you are satisfied with the location, make two small stitches with black embroidery floss for each eye.

RESOURCE GUIDE FOR PURCHASING MATERIALS

England

MOTHER GOOSE
10a Market Street
Nailsworth
Stroud
Gloucestershire, GL6 0BX
Tel: +44 (01453) 298725
www.mothergooseonline.co.uk

**MYRIAD NATURAL TOYS AND
CRAFTS**
Old Stable
Nine Yews
Cranborne
Dorset, BH21 5PW
Tel: +44 (01725) 517085 or
+44 (01725) 517040
www.myriadonline.co.uk

Wooden doll bases (conical figures), wool felt,
needle-felting materials, waxed kite paper,
paints and colored pencils.

Australia

EPOCHE
77 Monbulk Road
Kallista
Victoria 3791
Tel: +61 (03) 9755 1952
www.epoche.com.au

Natural crafting supplies.

MORNING STAR CRAFTS
Tel: +61 (03) 5985 6797
www.morningstarcrafts.com.au

Wool felt, needle-felting supplies, wooden
doll bases, waxed kite paper, watercolor
paints, colored pencils and natural beeswax.

WINTERWOOD TOYS
9 Colman Road
Warranwood
Victoria 3134
Tel: +61 (03) 9879 0426
www.winterwoodtoys.com

Wooden doll bases, wool felt, needle-felting
supplies, waxed kite paper, paints and
colored pencils.

Canada

BEAR DANCE CRAFTS
Tel: +1 (250) 353 2220
www.beardancecrafts.com

Wooden doll bases, wool felt and needle-
felting supplies.

BEAR WOODS SUPPLY CO., INC
Tel: +1 (800) 565 5066
www.woodparts.ca

MAPLEROSE
265 Baker Street
Nelson, BC
V1L 4H4
Tel: +1 (250) 352 5729

www.maplerose.ca

Wooden doll bases, wool felt and needle-
felting supplies, waxed kite paper, paints and
colored pencils, beeswax.

USA

BELLA LUNA TOYS
Tel: +1 (888) 438 1299
www.bellalunatoys.com

Wooden doll bases, wool felt and needle-
felting supplies, waxed kite paper, paints and
colored pencils, beeswax.

CASEY'S WOOD
Tel: +1 (800) 452 2739
www.caseyswood.com

Doll bases (peg people), candle cups, and an
assortment of other wonderful and useful
wooden pieces. Note: Casey's Wood will ship
their wood products internationally.

A CHILD'S DREAM COME TRUE
214-A Cedar Street
Sandpoint
Idaho 83864
Tel: +1 (208) 255 1664
www.achildsdream.com

Wool felt, needle-felting supplies, waxed kite
paper, paints and colored pencils, wooden doll
bases.

NOVA NATURAL
Tel: +1 (877) 668 2111
www.novanatural.com

Wool felt, needle-felting supplies, waxed kite
paper, paints and colored pencils, beeswax.

WOODWORKS LTD
4521 Anderson Boulevard
Haltom City
TX 76117
Tel: +1 (800) 722 0311 or
+1 (817) 581 5230
www.craftparts.com

Wooden peg doll bases and a wide assortment
of other wooden shapes and pieces. Note:
Woodworks will ship their wood products
internationally.

....

Etsy
www.etsy.com

Etsy is an online, global marketplace where
vendors sell finished craft items as well
as craft supplies. Wooden doll bases, wool
felt and needle-felting materials can all
be purchased from numerous suppliers
on Etsy; in addition, speciality and hard-
to-find items are available within this
marketplace. Etsy is also the best place to
acquire millinery flower stamens (which can
be used for butterfly and firefly antennae)
and vintage millinery flowers (used for the
wedding cake toppers in this book).

ACKNOWLEDGEMENTS

Author's Acknowledgements

Thank you to my parents who have shown me love in so many ways; to Samuel & Lev, my noisy muses; and to Paul because, wherever you are, that's my home. Thank you to Willow & Melainey Walker for sharing your heartfelt story; to Rachel Wolf for all kinds of inspiration (and for allowing me to use your idea for the zipper-pull); to Kristen Rettig, Caroline Spinali & Emily Smith, pattern-testers *extraordinaire*; and to wonderful friends, near and far, with whom I can consult regarding important topics such as favorite fairy-conveyances (you know who you are!). Thank you to Vandana & Keshav, Jasmine & Alexandra, Jack & Sam, Mikayla & Hudson, to little Shu, and to all their families for their generosity and time; to Anette Grostad for contributing your beautiful artwork; to Cornelia Funke for kind permission to use the excerpt from *Dragon Rider* on page 89; and finally to Lucy Guenot, Claire Percival, Olivia Desborough & Martin Large at Hawthorn Press for making this book possible.

www.webloomhere.blogspot.com

Margaret Bloom lives with her family in a small cottage beneath the great oak trees of Northern California. She has a Master's Degree in Counseling Psychology, and when she is not busy reading to her children, buttering toast or searching for lost socks, she spends her time writing, creating and finding inspiration in the world around her.

Other Books by Hawthorn Press

Making Peg Dolls
Margaret Bloom

Coming from the Waldorf handcraft tradition, these irresistible dolls encourage creative play and promote the emotional and imaginative development of young children. Peg dolls can be made from natural materials to reflect the seasonal cycle, favourite fairytales and festivals from around the world. Includes easy to follow, step-by-step instructions for children and crafters of all levels and experience, beautiful colour illustrations and photos, a range of over 60 designs and patterns for peg dolls and an inspiring section on storytelling with peg dolls.
192pp; 198 x 208mm; hardback; 978-1-907359-17-0

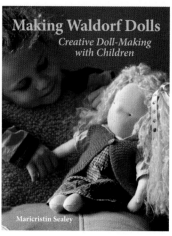

Making Waldorf Dolls
Creative doll-making with children
Maricristin Sealey

This comprehensive, well-illustrated book will give even the most nervous beginner the confidence to produce a unique, handcrafted toy from natural materials. Once you have mastered the basic baby dolls, you can progress to a more ambitious limbed or jointed doll. Contents include: ten designs including soft, baggy, pouch, angel, sack and limbed dolls; instructions for knitted, sewn and embroidered hairstyles; patterns for dolls' clothes and accessories; help with tools, techniques and materials; ideas for recycling clothing for dollmaking; where to get materials.
160pp; 246 x 189mm; paperback; 978-1-903458-58-7

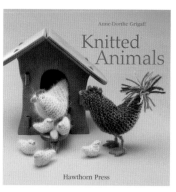

Knitted Animals
Anne-Dorthe Grigaff

Here is an irresistible collection of animals to knit in soft, natural materials: ducklings, teddy bears, lambs, piglets, hedgehogs, a handsome rooster, and many more. Most of the projects can be quickly and cheaply knitted with small oddments of wool, and many can be completed in an hour or two – ideal for knitters looking for ways to reduce their yarn stash! Contents include: step-by-step instructions for making over 20 delightful knitted animals; beautiful colour photography throughout; a good range of projects suitable for older children with basic knitting skills; finished designs that make enchanting children's toys and gifts.
64pp; 198 x 208mm; hardback; 978-1-903458-68-6

Making Woodland Crafts
Using green sticks, rods, poles, beads and string
Patrick Harrison

Through a series of visually stunning hand-drawn illustrations, *Making Woodland Crafts* guides the reader on making things in the woods. This book provides the basic knowledge and skills to complete a range of both simple and more advanced craft projects, from functional structures to creative outdoor play forms. You'll learn to choose and work your wood effectively, use simple tools, tie knots and develop your own designs to make masks and puppets, night torches and staffs, arrows, jewellery, ladders, shelters, chairs for stargazing and much more. This book will teach you all you need to know to make working with wood fun for parents, teachers and children. Step-by-step instructions throughout.
128pp; 198 x 208mm; hardback; 978-1-907359-37-8

Baking Bread with Children
Warren Lee Cohen

Baking Bread with Children has everything you need to share the magic of baking with children of all ages. The techniques and recipes are cleverly seasoned with stories, songs and poems to make the whole process really enjoyable for everyone. There are also instructions for building and using a bread oven, baking projects for kindergarten and school, and useful nutritional information.
'This delightful cornucopia extends an invitation to share the magic of baking bread with children of all ages ... Information about the seven different grains, wheat sensitivities, allergies and coeliac disease is presented clearly. Bread projects and educational activities includes 12 steps to building and firing your own earthen bread oven.' Montessori International
128pp; 250 x 200mm; paperback; 978-1-903458-60-0

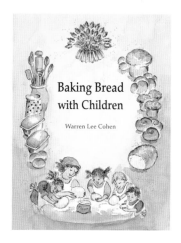

Puppet Theatre
Maija Baric

Puppet Theatre offers twelve detailed, beautifully illustrated projects with all the techniques you need for a simple puppet show or full theatrical performance. You can make finger, hand and knee puppets; make puppets from twigs, stones, potatoes and paper; construct rod puppets, marionettes and shadow theatre; animate your puppets and give each their own unique character; create costumes, staging, scenery, props, lighting and sound effects.
'This book is fantastic! .... Children of all ages will adore this book due to the lively pictures that accompany the writing and fill every page.' Deborah Fullwood, Playwords
96pp; 210 x 260mm; hardback; 978-1-903458-72-3

Findus Food and Fun
Seasonal crafts, recipes and nature activities
Sven Nordqvist, Eva-Lena Larsson, Kennart Danielsson

Pettson, Findus and the muckles have gathered together a whole year's worth of indoor and outdoor activities that can be done using things from around the house. For each month there is something new that can be discovered and explored, invented and made, grown or baked. Beautifully illustrated and clearly explained, this craft activity book will keep curious children and adults occupied and enchanted all year round.
64pp; 297 x 210mm; hardback; 978-1-907359-34-7

All Year Round
A calendar of celebration
Ann Druitt, Christine Fynes-Clinton, Marije Rowling

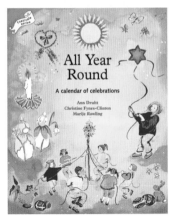

All Year Round is brimming with things to make, activities, stories, poems and songs to share with your family. It is full of well-illustrated ideas for fun and celebration: Observing the round of festivals is an enjoyable way to bring rhythm into children's lives and provide a series of meaningful landmarks to look forward to. Each festival has a special character of its own: participation can deepen our understanding and love of nature and bring a gift to the whole family.

'Delightful illustrations, hundreds of things to make, recipes to enjoy and songs to share, make this book a real family treasury.' The Green Parent
320pp; 250 x 200mm; paperback; 978-1-869891-47-6

Games Children Sing and Play
Singing movement games to play with children ages 3–5
Joan Carr Shimer, Valerie Baadh Garrett

Illustrated in full colour throughout, this treasury comprises both traditional gems and also new games to help children feel at ease in their bodies and build relationships with others. Contents include: how games help child development and physical coordination; tips for using the games with children; how healthy movement helps children's learning; how movement games help develop the senses; 34 singing and movement games.

'This book reminds us of the beauty and power of living song and movement. It will nourish children and adults alike as they share the music together.'
Joan Almon, Alliance for Childhood
112pp; 200 x 250mm; paperback; 978-1-907359-20-0

Old Freedom Train
A Waldorf inspired alphabet
Shayne Jackman

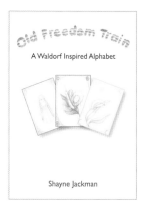

Old Freedom Train takes children on a magical journey through the letters of the alphabet, rather than just introducing the letters just as abstract symbols. Each picture is a letter and each letter is a picture, with verses to match. Letters are characterised and enlivened by pictures and beautiful verse drawn from songs, nursery rhymes and poems. This helps children imagine and experience letters creatively with both head and heart.

'We used Old Freedom Train to help my son learn the alphabet... it took us on a wonderful learning journey with its beautiful illustrations and lovely accompanying verses.' Alison Terry, Australia

60pp; 297 x 210mm; hardback; 978-1-907359-40-8

Making the Children's Year
Seasonal Waldorf Crafts with Children
Marije Rowling

Marije has completely revised the book she originally co-wrote with two friends, bringing new inspiration and ideas to a modern readership. Now with beautiful colour illustrations, and packed with all kinds of crafts, from papercrafting to building dens, this book brings the seasons into the home. From beginners to experienced crafters, here is a gift for parents and adults seeking to make toys that will inspire children and provide an alternative to throwaway cult

240pp; 250 x 200mm; paperback; 978-1-907359-69-9

Making Needle-Felted Animals
Steffi Stern & Sophie Buckley

Written by experienced crafters and workshop leaders, this book is an essential guide for anyone interested in the popular craft of needle-felting. Requiring no experience, the projects progressively build on skills throughout and will transform you into an avid needle-felter in no time at all. Inspired by the natural world, the projects aim to engage us in, and re-connect us more fully to, the worlds of art, imagination, play and nature. With 20 patterns and design ideas for creating your own needle-felted animals, this practical guide highlights common mistakes, offers creative solutions to fix them, and also includes includes poems, stories and songs.

112pp; 198 x 208mm; paperback; 978-1-907359-46-0

Ordering Books

If you have difficulties ordering Hawthorn Press books from a bookshop, you can order direct from our website **www.hawthornpress.com** or from the following distributors:

UK
BookSource
50 Cambuslang Road
Glasgow, G32 8NB
Tel: (0845) 370 0063
Email: orders@booksource.net

USA
Steinerbooks
PO Box 960, Herndon
VA 20171-0960
Tel: (800) 856 8664
Email: service@steinerbooks.org

CANADA
Trifold Books
PO Box 32, Guelph
Ontario, NIH 6J6
Tel: (519) 821 9901
Email: info@trifoldbooks.com

AUSTRALIA
Footprint Books
1/6a Prosperity Parade
Warriewood
NSW 2102
Tel: (02) 9997 3973
Email: info@footprint.com.au
www.footprint.com.au

NEW ZEALAND
Ceres Books
Ceres Enterprises Ltd
82 Carbine Road
Mt Wellington, Auckland
Tel: (64) 9574 3356
Email: info@ceresbooks.co.nz
www.ceresbooks.co.nz

EUROPE
Contact Saltway Publishing for information on European stockists.
Email: chris.mclaren@saltwaypublishing.co.uk

Hawthorn Press

www.hawthornpress.com